Kitchens

CANCELLED

Kitchens

a design source book

RYLAND
PETERS
& SMALL

LONDON NEW YORK

Vinny Lee

with photography by
James Merrell

Stylist   **Cynthia Inions**

For this edition:
Senior designer   Sally Powell
Senior editor   Henrietta Heald
Picture research   Emily Westlake
Production   Gavin Bradshaw
Art director   Gabriella Le Grazie
Publishing director   Alison Starling

To AWJ, my companion in life's steamy kitchen

First published in the United Kingdom in 1998
and reissued with amendments in 2005
by Ryland Peters & Small
20–21 Jockey's Fields, London WC1R 4BW

Text © Vinny Lee 1998, 2005
Design and photographs © Ryland Peters & Small 1998, 2005

ISBN 1 84172 927 2

A CIP record for this book is available from the British Library.

Printed in China.

contents

introduction

Over the last thirty or forty years the kitchen has become the centre of the home. No longer reserved purely for the storage and preparation of food, it now often serves as a dining room, family room or laundry as well. Many other demands are made on the space: its roles range from providing basic essentials such as fire and water to accommodating a whole host of labour-saving machines and gadgets.

The purpose and nature of cooking itself now goes far beyond the supply of sustenance. Recipes, ingredients and styles of cookery from around the world have hugely increased the home cook's repertoire. Woks, steamers, rice cookers, ice-cream machines and pasta makers are now found in households far beyond their native countries. Pre-prepared and 'instant' foods are increasingly popular in busy households, with the result that the microwave oven has grown in importance, sometimes replacing the conventional cooker.

Kitchen styles, like clothes fashions, take inspiration from a whole range of sources, from the colourful richness of Mediterranean farmhouses to the high-tech streamlined designs of the steel-clad professional kitchen. Nostalgia is a perennial influence: period styles, such as Victorian, 1950s or Gothic, are often adapted to suit the plans, requirements and modern gadgetry of today's kitchen.

The development of new laminates and materials has also seen the kitchen become a more colourful and fashionable room. No longer restricted to practical wipe-clean ceramic tiles and gloss paintwork, decorative options now include specially finished non-rust metals, reinforced, sandblasted and etched glass, coloured woods and plastic. New seals

Left A kitchen may be part of an open-plan space which includes living and dining functions, in which case the layout and design of the kitchen will be an integral part of the whole room scheme.

Below **Tried and tested utensils never go out of date. A sturdy good-sized wooden chopping board and a robust enamel jug are classics that still find their place in the modern kitchen.**
Right **Keeping the storage element of this kitchen at a low level makes the linear layout appear more spacious and uncluttered, and gives the room the appearance of height.**

and finishes mean that traditional materials, such as slate and wood, can be made more durable and resilient to daily wear and tear.

Whether you are designing a kitchen from scratch, renovating an old one or reorganizing an existing one, start by deciding exactly what you want – but remain open to the advice of professional experts, especially in technical areas such as installation, plumbing and wiring. Updating a scheme can be as simple as buying new accessories or changing unit doors, but if you are undertaking extensive changes or the installation of a new kitchen, there are many things to consider before embarking on the project, including practical, safety and hygiene standards and requirements – to say nothing of cost. If you are working to a strict budget, be aware of extra expenses that may arise and create a contingency fund.

Technical advances in equipment are constant and fast-moving, so make time to browse around major kitchen appliance shops or department stores to see what's new. There are fashions in gadgets and machines – the trendiest ones may have an instant appeal but soon find their way into the obsolete or rarely used drawer or quickly become dated. Longevity and durability should be top priorites when buying kitchen equipment.

Don't be easily seduced by fashionable kitchen styles – think of the practicalities. Some of the high-tech professional-style kitchens are fine if you have a battery of *sous-chefs* and staff to scrub down the surfaces and clean the place from top to toe each day, but, if you are on your own, keeping the shining steel surfaces clean can be an overwhelming task. Also, large industrial cookers are likely to have large pan supports designed to take commercial equipment, and an omelette pan designed for one person will fall through the gaps. Even the more traditional style of kitchen, with pots and pans hanging from beams or rafters, is prone to suffer from an accumulation of grease and the odd splash of sauce or fat, so hang pots and pans away from worksurfaces where frying and cooking takes place and you will reduce the cleaning time after each meal.

When embarking on planning or replanning a kitchen, resolve to create a room that suits your lifestyle as well as your style aspirations. But, above all, make sure that the kitchen you end up with is a room where you feel at home. It should not only be a place that is practical and comfortable to work in but also a haven where your friends feel welcome to come and chat while you cook, to drink coffee and gossip. The kitchen is no longer a place of toil and labour – it is often the most sociable and frequently used room in a home, so it should be one that can be enjoyed on many levels.

first **pri**

nciples

planning and design

fitting and installing

introduction

When you have decided that you need a new kitchen, or that your existing one needs updating, where and how do you start? Don't rush in thinking that a few cupboards and a couple of machines will suffice, they won't – it takes time and effort to create a well-designed practical layout. A kitchen is a functional space and one that requires a certain amount of financial commitment. Expenditure is needed for both materials and equipment, but it is money that, spent well, will be an investment for years to come.

A good kitchen is said to add value to a property, but it is the room that a new purchaser will most often change, whether cosmetically with new paint and tiles or dramatically with a re-plan and new units. The amount of investment you make in your kitchen will depend on whether you plan to stay in the home for a considerable period or whether it is a short-term residence. A kitchen in the second category will need to be a good, safe workplace but should be decorated in neutral or low-key colours and with fittings that are classic rather than too fashionable or idiosyncratic, so that they will encourage rather than put off a potential purchaser.

Planning is the most important part of installing a kitchen. Spending time and effort on this initial stage will save headaches later on. Working with an architect or professional planner can make the task easier but it is important to know what you want, and to be aware of the vast range of products and finishes available. No one expects you to become an instant expert but the more groundwork and research you do the more options you give yourself. Whether the kitchen is fitted or unfitted, the three basic requirements are a heat source, a supply of water and cold storage. Around these you can add storage for food, china and cutlery, worktops on which to prepare food, then the secondary electrical and plumbing requirements such as waste disposal, dishwasher, plugs and sockets, lighting and so on. Once these have been allocated a position and the basic functioning of the kitchen worked out, then the 'dressings' – the colours and finishes – can be planned and discussed.

Think of the process like a body. The form and function of the kitchen is like the skeleton – this has to be fine tuned before the outer layers are added. If the skeleton is badly adjusted, then no matter how fine and expensive the dressings are the thing will fail to function properly. With the elements of fire and water combined in the kitchen there are inherent dangers, so good installation is vital to avoid accidents.

Opposite **Smooth, unobtrusive lines and well-planned preparation and storage areas are essential in a practical working kitchen. Getting the basics right is the key to a successful result.**

planning
and design

The first and most important thing to get clear in your mind is what you want from your kitchen. Define the purpose of the space and how often it will be used. Look at your lifestyle and circumstances. Do you live alone? Are you a professional couple without children? Or are you a family with children? And how many people will be using the kitchen on a regular basis?

Next, gauge how often it will be used and how much storage space will be needed. The questions that will help you get these answers are: do you enjoy cooking and entertaining or do you tend to buy ready-prepared foods or eat out a lot? If you entertain, how many people do you have on average – mostly small suppers for four or six or grand dinners for ten to twelve? Do you usually shop on a daily or a weekly or a monthly basis? Is food storage to be for mainly fresh produce or for frozen and tinned goods? This will give you an idea of how much dry or shelf storage you should allow for and how big a fridge you might need.

It is important to have an accurate idea of the expected use of the kitchen. For example, an urban-dwelling, busy professional couple who have the occasional pasta or pre-prepared meal at home will not require the same size of kitchen or as much storage space as the family with three small children who live in the country and eat most meals at home. Is the area to be used solely for food preparation and cooking or is the kitchen area part of a room with another purpose? For example, will the space be used for family and friends to sit around and talk, watch television and relax? Is the kitchen also a laundry area, with a washing machine or tumble drier installed?

Assess the dimensions and the pros and cons of the area. This will give you a clear understanding of the layout and advantages and disadvantages of the space. How many doors are there? Do they open in or out and are all of them needed? Are there any unusual pillars, chimney breasts or features that cause the walls to be irregular rather than flat? If the room is small can other

Left **When planning a kitchen your aim is to create a welcoming place.**
Above **Consider many different types of storage for versatility.**
Top right **A table top provides multi-purpose work and dining space.**
Right **Remember the kitchen must be functioning as well as look good: it will not remain immaculate!**

functions such as the laundry be moved elsewhere, say into the bathroom or a hall or passageway? Is there any feasible way of extending the space, by knocking through into another room, re-arranging the space or adding an extension such as a conservatory? If so, do you have the budget for this sort of building work as well as fitting the kitchen or will you have to use the space you have to the best advantage? If this is the case, try to think of a scheme that will optimize the space you have.

When planning a small kitchen draw inspiration from similar sized areas such as a ship's galley or a caravan or mobile home. In these situations the wall space is utilized with half shelves fitted under overhead cupboards but still giving access to the worktop. Overhead hanging rails, from which utensils can be hung, are also space saving, but make sure that they are positioned in a place where you are not likely to bump into them, ideally under shelves or over a central unit.

Finally, look around and see how much natural light there is in the room. If there is little or none consider ways of obtaining or increasing the amount of daylight through the installation of a roof skylight or french doors. Also look to see if there is access to outside walls for ducting. This is particularly important in flats or loft apartments where kitchens may be sited in the interior of the building. Machines such as extractors and tumble driers require an outer wall for their exit pipes. This

can, in some cases, be done through other ducting routes but it may be expensive to install these and they may be obtrusive. Locate the waste outlets and water pipes also, as these will indicate where major plumbing, such as the sink and dishwasher, should ideally be installed.

Making a plan

When you have drawn up a comprehensive list of all the functions that will take place in the room it is time to start manipulating the space available to accommodate them. The easiest way to do this is to draw a scale outline of the kitchen on squared or graph paper. Installing a kitchen is a serious and permanent investment so it is worth taking time to try various plans and schemes before deciding on the final layout. The paper plan is the easiest way to try different combinations on your own, but if you have access to a computer and suitable software a design programme is the quickest way to generate accurate plans. You could also discuss your ideas with a professional kitchen planner, and some manufacturers may be able to show you similar layouts in their own showrooms. It can be very difficult to visualize how units, colours and schemes will look in reality and it is hard to predict and accommodate every mistake or oversight that may occur in the fitting stage, but try to pre-empt as much as you can as it will, in the long term, save you time and money.

Top left **Storage space is important. A plate rack can be used to hold china as well as allow it to drip dry over a draining board or sink.**

Top centre **Smaller items of foodstuffs and utensils can get lost on open shelving so store them in larger containers that are attractive enough to put on display: a wicker basket is ideal for keeping vegetables because air circulates through it.**

Top right **Items used frequently should be stored close to hand so that you do not have to waste time searching for them.**

Above and opposite **Basic open shelves provide good storage as items are easily seen and can be immediately identified.**

A wall of superbly crafted cupboards conceals all the paraphernalia of the kitchen – from china and glass to fridges and comestibles. When closed the cupboards appear to be a panelled wall, but behind this façade is well-planned and spacious storage. This type of arrangement is ideal in a kitchen/dining area where formal entertaining takes place.

Left and above **The walls that enclosed this kitchen have been stripped out to make it part of the main living area. Given definition by its distinct flooring and the large overhead lighting panel, the kitchen is compact but also highly efficient. The sense of space is increased by glimpses of rooms beyond.**
Top left and centre **Light floods through an internal window to illuminate this tiny kitchen. The hinged sink cover, which can be lowered to create a work surface, is an ingenious space-saving solution.**
Top right **Three small rooms have been combined to make one generous kitchen, incorporating existing recesses. The tiled surfaces set a tone of old-fashioned practicality, while the steel-and-glass cupboard doors add contemporary sparkle.**
Opposite **The smooth and polished concrete floor makes an effective counterpoint to the substantial wooden beams, clean lines and metal finishes in this industrial-style kitchen.**

Plot in the general shape of the room on your paper or computer plan, and then add in features such as windows, doors, hot and cold water pipes, electrical power points and radiators (although these can be moved it is worth putting them in to give yourself an idea of where plumbing and electrician costs may occur). Try to keep windows free of overhead units or anything that may block the light. In front of a window is a good place to have a chopping board or a worktop so that food preparation can be carried out in maximum light. When marking in where the doors and windows are, note how they open as this may affect access to cupboards. For example, if the room door opens flat against a cupboard door then it may be difficult to get into the cupboard.

Choosing appliances

If you have existing appliances or furniture that will be used again, draw the items to scale on another piece of paper, then cut them out and label them. Do the same for any new pieces of equipment you are thinking of buying. This is the time to think carefully about the size and capacity of the machines you

want to buy. If you use your fridge for storing most of your food, you can probably sacrifice dry or shelf storage space to accommodate a big machine, but if you really only keep salad stuff and milk in the fridge allow more shelf and cupboard space for tinned or packet foods.

If you live alone, eat breakfast on the way to work and only have a couple of friends over once a month for a bowl of soup and a cheese sandwich then a dishwasher with a twenty place setting capacity is not for you. What you probably want is a small machine with six settings which can be run through twice to cope with a busy evening. Is a twin sink and double drainer necessary if you have a dishwasher? Would a single sink and one drainer suffice?

Similar analysis should also be used when buying a cooker. If you do not like cooking, do you actually need a cooker or would a hob and a microwave cover your requirements? The six-ring, double oven industrial cooker may look wonderful in the showroom and in magazine articles but in reality will you use all six rings and both ovens or would a smaller version be more practical? Find out the dimensions of the equipment you are planning to buy and again make

Left **The surfaces near the cooker or hob should, ideally, be heat resistant so that hot plates or pots can be put down quickly and easily when they are being taken out of the oven or removed from the heat of a burner.**

Below **Steel is a good heat resistant surface but it also makes an excellent general worktop. It can be quickly cooled down with cold water or ice which makes it, like marble, useful for pastry preparation. Usually seam free, steel is also easy to wipe clean and devoid of ridges and niches where grime might collect.**

scale drawings. Place the cut-outs of all the equipment and furniture on the floor plan and try to make them fit. You may find that you need to compromise and opt for a smaller machine or a different configuration. For example, you may find that the double oven you wanted is too big for the area you have and that a wall-mounted oven and separate hob would be better. Or that the cooker can be accommodated but the combined fridge-freezer will have to be two separate smaller units that sit side by side. When you are trying this manipulation of space and machines keep a list of alternative equipment by you, with designs and sizes that provide a similar capacity or function.

The work triangle

A rule-of-thumb guide to planning a kitchen is to use what is known as the work triangle. The theory is that the main work areas – the sink, the hob or cooker and fridge – should be sited so that they form an imaginary triangle. This provides the most efficient use of space and time. For example, in the course of the preparation of a meal you would get the ingredients from the fridge, take them to the sink to wash them and then turn to the hob or oven to cook them, so in an ideal plan these three work stations should be within easy reach of each other. It is also worth taking into consideration where the main flow of traffic through the kitchen will be. Ideally the work triangle should not be in the middle of this area as accidents may occur when people cross through. The

area where people come to or from a table or eating area should also be away from the oven. Consider also the inclusion of worktop space on either side of the hob or oven so that hot or heavy dishes can be put down quickly and safely. Keep appliances of similar function together, for example the washing machine next to the tumble drier, and the dishwasher near the sink, for easy plumbing, but also near cupboards where everyday china, glass and cutlery are stored – this will cut down on the amount of lifting and carrying that has to be done.

As a general rule there should be a panel between a fridge-freezer and cooker to prevent the heat from the cooker affecting the efficiency of the fridge, although most modern fridges are now well insulated. Also, allow plenty of space for machine doors to open. Dishwasher doors which generally open from top to bottom require more room because you have to stand in front or to the side of the door to fill and empty the machine; the same applies to opening front-loading washing machines. Fridge or cupboard doors which open right to left may not always need to be opened right back, so they take up less space.

Fitted or unfitted?

Once the appliances and equipment are in place on your plan then you can start filling in the remaining areas with storage space and worktops. At this point you have to address the question of whether a fitted or an unfitted kitchen is the best option. This is also a matter of taste: some people prefer

Left **If you are planning to place a fridge-freezer next to a powerful cooker check with the manufacturers or suppliers of both appliances that the fridge mechanism will not be affected by the heat that is output by the cooker and the hob. If there is likely to be a problem, securing a heat-proof insulation panel between the fridge and the cooker will help prevent defrosting or damage to the fridge exterior.**
Below left **Having a wipe-clean rim or resting area around the edge of a hob or grill is useful for putting down dripping or hot spoons or utensils.**

the tailored lines of the fitted kitchen while others opt for the versatility and flexibility of the unfitted variety. In a smaller kitchen, fitted units are often the best option because they can be planned and installed to use every available inch of space. But the advantage of freestanding, unfitted units is that you can take them with you when you move. This means that it is worth investing in more expensive pieces of furniture because you will get longer use from them. If you are living in temporary accommodation such as a rented flat, good quality freestanding units will look good, give you pleasure and travel with you when you leave your current address. With unfitted furniture you can take your time and gradually build up your kitchen, getting to know the room and your requirements before adding the next unit. It also means that you can spread the cost over months or years rather than having to commit a substantial amount of money all in one go, as you would when buying a fitted design.

Mixing and matching units can also create an interesting look. Antique pine dressers alongside a steel-topped workbench will bring together old and new in a way that a pre-planned fitted kitchen may not achieve. This sort of arrangement is also versatile – for example, if a dresser or chest is no longer needed in the kitchen it can be moved to another room and become a linen closet for towels and bedclothes. You can also make a virtue out of having a mix-and-match collection of units. You could opt for a rainbow range of colours rather than trying to conform to a regular or limited scheme. Paint each piece of furniture a different shade of the same colour, or with a spectrum of colours, then go the whole way and add different knobs and door handles so that the eclectic appearance is carried all the way through. A decorative splashback in a harlequin mix of coloured ceramic tiles could complete the bohemian look.

Mobile furniture

In an unfitted kitchen heavier units should ideally be mounted on wheels or castors so that they can be easily moved away from the wall for cleaning or re-decorating. It is important to ensure that the unit is level and sturdy so that it will not topple or fall over – this is especially important with larger units. If you add castors or wheels try to fix the type that have lever breaks so that the unit can be well-stabilized when in position.

Mobile furniture may also be used to create different settings or emphasis in a room. For example, if you cook and entertain in the same place, a lightweight bookcase with a solid back, filled with a few choice books and pieces of china might be wheeled in front of a work surface (don't overburden it or it will be heavy and difficult to move). This will create a temporary wall between the cooking and eating areas, then it can be pushed back against the

Right **The overhanging section at the end of the main kitchen unit provides a surface for breakfast and snacks, while more formal meals are taken around the long table in the foreground.**
Below **Huge windows allow plenty of light to enter this simply decorated kitchen, although additional task lighting will be required.**
Opposite **The warm tones and vertical figuring of the wooden units and flooring add colour and pattern, as well as creating a grounding effect.**

wall when not needed. Butcher's blocks are useful because they can be stored under the worktop or in a corner but brought out to provide extra preparation space. Vegetable baskets are similarly adaptable; they can be brought out when shopping is being unpacked then rolled back into their storage area, or taken to the sink for vegetables to be removed for washing and preparation.

For people who spend time in the kitchen and prepare food from scratch, it is important that units and appliances are at the correct height. The function of the kitchen sink is now mainly replaced by the dishwasher, but vegetables and pots and pans, as well as valuable china and delicate crystal glasses, are still washed by hand. Stooping over a low sink or stretching up to a tall worktop can be laborious and is likely to cause accidents so make sure that the base of the sink or height of the worktop is at a comfortable level. A mix of mid-height and taller units will make it possible for a couple who are of notably different heights to work without incurring backache from leaning over or stretching beyond their natural reach. Eye-level grills should also be at eye-level – if not it is difficult to watch food being cooked and you may burn your hand on the grill when the grill pan is being removed. So make sure that the kitchen is fitted to suit *your* height and eye-level rather than that of the 'average' person.

A multi-function kitchen

If you plan to use your kitchen in different ways it is best to think of the room divided into sections. Assign an area for cooking and food preparation, another for eating and a third for sitting and relaxing. Ideally there should be a logical order to the layout so that when the food is ready to eat it can be quickly and easily transferred to the table in the eating area. The seating area should be furthest away from the food preparation section, so that when the work is done the kitchen can be cleared and the lights turned off. It is also safer to take hot dishes directly to the dining area instead of walking through a busy living area.

If the room is too small to subdivide into three separate areas, subtract or condense the functions until you can allow comfortable space for each one. For example, an island unit or peninsular worktop without overhead cupboards could double as an dining table with high stools and still create a barrier between cooking and seating areas. The eating space that doubles as a living area should have chairs that are comfortable enough to linger in after a meal, with a table that is at a good height to do homework or other pastimes. Or a foldaway table and chairs could be used for dining, then put away when not in use, and armchairs on castors could be pushed to the outer edges of the room when meals are in progress. Alternatively, the living and dining functions could be combined by having an adjustable table that can be raised when you are eating or lowered to coffee-table height when you are relaxing.

fitting and installing

Unless you are a very talented and competent DIY expert the installation of a kitchen is something best left to the professionals, but it is worth knowing the basics and a little about the work involved so you can be prepared for what is to come. Being acquainted with the basic schedule will also help you have things ready as and when they are needed. For example, finding the right tiles should take preference over a wall-mounted spice rack which will not be fitted until after the tiles are in place. Keeping your eyes open and being involved in the installation may also help you notice hitches and problems as they happen so that they can be solved while the work is in progress rather than at a later date when the units are secured and tiles and worktops are fixed in place.

Once you have more or less decided on your kitchen plan, then it is time to gather quotations from builders, kitchen fitters, plumbers and electricians to keep a focus on how much it is likely to cost and to make sure that you are still within your budget. It is worth getting a couple of quotes so you can compare prices, and if one is far lower or far higher than another ask why the difference is so radical. The explanation may help you choose one workman above another. Also ask for references – someone who has experience of their work before may provide you with useful information. If you are buying your own units and major appliances check with the installer as to whether they can get the items more cheaply. People in the trade can often buy items at wholesale prices and may be prepared to buy the item through a trade-only outlet if they are commissioned to fit and install the item in your home.

If you are arranging your own installation plan to do it in a logical order. For example, it is best to have electrical wiring, say for recessed ceiling lights and wall sockets, done before the plastering and tiling are in place. It is better to have the units and machines installed after the floor has been laid so that they can rest on top of the flooring rather than have tiles or linoleum butting up to the edge of the unit. If the line is fitted to the edge, rather than under the unit, it may peel back in time, but the weight of the machine or unit will help anchor the flooring in place. It may also be worth having most of the paintwork done before the units are fitted so that there is less danger of paint being splashed on them. Although the process of fitting units may incur scuffs or scratches these can be touched up later when all the fitting is completed.

Fitting units

Once you have decided on the layout of the kitchen, where the machines will go and how the units should be placed it is time to get down to the basics. If your kitchen is to be custom made then you will have cupboards designed and fitted to suit your room. With an unfitted kitchen you have more flexibility but the size and shape of the furniture will still be influenced by the capacity and angles of the kitchen. If you choose a commercially produced, standard

Left **Smooth running drawers are the sign of a well fitted kitchen.**
Top right **An apparently unsupported bench provides extra work surface but does not block out light.**
Right **Adjustable shelving is good in units where you keep lightweight goods. For heavier equipment fixed shelves are a more sturdy option.**

kitchen then you will have to consider how the pre-made cupboard units, known as carcasses, can be adapted to suit your needs and the dimensions of your room. Very few kitchens are perfectly symmetrical and fewer still will be just the right size to accommodate an exact number of pre-fabricated cupboards, which come in fixed sizes. There are two basic types of units used in fitted kitchens, these are base and wall mounted. Fill-in units such as a tall broom type cupboard may also be available as standard but not all manufacturers supply them. Most mass-produced cupboard carcasses are made from chipboard, plywood or MDF with a standard melamine finish.

Internally they may have fitted, rigid shelves or adjustable ones that can be moved up and down on a peg and socket fitting. Other units will have a single drawer above a smaller cupboard space or be fitted with a set of drawers. Most units have adjustable legs which will be concealed, when the unit is secured, by kickboard panels fitted to the base of the unit. These units are almost all standard in shape and construction but it is the doors, whether from a stock range or custom made, that give the kitchen its character and style.

Think carefully about the combination and location of these units so that drawers for cutlery and cloths are near the area where they will be needed and the shelves for storage will be in an area where they are accessible. For example, it is usually wise to have a shelf-free cupboard under the sink so that you can keep detergents and dishwashing fluids together in that space and away

Above **A built-in bench provides more seating space than could have been achieved with individual chairs.**
Right **This combination of fitted and unfitted furniture creates an informal but smart appearance.**

from food stuffs which might be tainted by scents or soapy flavours. Also, plan to put heavier pans and equipment in base cupboards rather than in wall-mounted ones where too much weight may cause the cupboard to come away from the wall. Store lightweight china and glass in upper units.

Standard base and floor units can be placed so that they cover most of a wall, but gaps may occur where the wall is longer than the total length of the units. Instead of leaving a single large gap at the

Incorporate a balanced mix of fitted and freestanding units and appliances, with custom-made details such as plate racks or open shelving, for the most versatility.

end of the run of units, you might like to divide the space so that it occurs between groups of units. The gaps can then be used to insert a towel rail (if it is a small gap) or a wine rack (if larger), and a space between two wall-mounted units over the sink area is ideal for putting a plate rack. These 'left-over' spaces need not be wasted – in some cases, it is better to allow room for a few breaks in a block of units, especially in a large kitchen, to give breathing space to a continuous wall of single-coloured cupboards. Plate and wine racks can be bought ready-made, but again you may have trouble finding just the right size to accommodate the

space you have – it is like trying to find a missing piece of a jigsaw. To overcome this problem, you might want to employ a carpenter to custom-build these accessories. If you are working to a tight budget, you can buy the bulk of the kitchen units from a mass-produced range but use the professional skills of a carpenter to add the finishing touches and details that will make the kitchen unique.

The same applies to the decoration of the doors: you may choose carcasses from a standard range but have the doors custom made, or even buy plain wooden doors and have them painted or decorated to your personal taste, whether it be a simple colour wash or a more elaborate effect of cut-outs backed with a wire mesh or sandblasted patterned glass.

The positioning of unit doors themselves is also important. Instead of having all the doors opening in the same direction, usually from right to left, think about the option of having a left and right opening door beside each other so that you can have easy access to both cupboards at the same time – especially if you store long or large items there such as a fish kettle or paella pan. If both doors open to the left the second door will impede entry to the first cupboard. Corners are particularly difficult areas to fit successfully. Shelves

may be deep and difficult to reach into. In these spaces revolving metal or plastic shelves on a central pivot can make access easier. Also a set of open shelves for attractive large items, such as coloured enamel casseroles or stainless steel pots and pans can make practical use of an otherwise 'dead' area and as these items are large they will not be pushed to the back of the shelf.

If the floor is uneven, or the wall to which the unit is being attached is not level, the adjustable legs on the units will enable a certain amount of re-adjustment to be done. Having level base units is not only important for the look of the kitchen but will be essential when the worktop is fitted. The surface must be level so that things will not roll off and any unevenness may cause a continuous length of a melamine-topped chipboard or wood veneer worktop to bend and eventually break.

Worktops should be carefully fitted and once in place well sealed. The end edges of work surfaces should be capped off with a matching piece of laminate, or in the case of marble or granite polished to a smooth finish. In kitchens where the worktop

Above, left to right **Make sure that the type of storage you choose is sturdy enough to cope with the weight of the items to be stacked in or on it.** Opposite **The structural supports of the building are used as part of the storage and decoration of this room. Interesting features, such as these beams, can be incorporated into a scheme.**

may jut out into a thoroughfare it may be worth having the ends cut at an angle so that they taper to the wall and do not cause bruises to those who may bump into them when passing. Similar care should be taken when fitting overhead cupboards over an area where chores may be carried out and on the corners of extractor fans over hobs. If the fan casing is being constructed on site these details can be attended to during the assembly but if the casing is pre-made the corners may have to be sanded and rounded when it is delivered or capped off with plastic covers.

Plumbing and wiring

During installation take time to gauge the siting of electrical sockets before wall tiles or splashbacks are in place. Electrical equipment should be used far from the naked flames or heat of a hob or cooker and the sockets should be sited away from running water. These aspects should be discussed with the professional electrician who advises you on the wiring and installation of equipment in the kitchen. Sockets should also be placed near units where machines are stored and over work surfaces where the machines will be used so that heavier items such as breadmakers and food processors do not have to be lifted and carried over distances. Ideally the socket should be placed at a height that allows the gadget to be readily used, but without lengths of flex cluttering the worktop. If you place the sockets correctly it may even be possible to reduce the length of flex on the machine, making it neater and more practical to use.

There are a variety of safety regulations that must be adhered to and these should be followed when your electrical fittings are installed. In the UK a Certificate of Occupancy, known as a CO, will not be issued on a new development or refurbishment unless the installations meet the code. Your local authority planning department may send an inspector to approve safety features and requirements before a building is given a certificate. To meet these standards, and for your own safety, it is best to employ a professional electrician and plumber to fit and wire sockets as well as larger machines, circuit breakers and high voltage power cables for cookers. Many professional bodies of craftsmen, such as builders and plumbers, issue their certified members with an insignia or seal so

that reputable tradesmen can be distinguished from 'cowboys'. These bodies may offer guarantees of craftsmanship and in some cases compensation or insurance against negligence, so when employing a person to do these jobs for you ask if they are affiliated to any recognized trade body.

Most of the new equipment that you buy will come with guarantees and warranties, but if you are renovating an existing kitchen or choose to buy second-hand equipment this paperwork may not be available. If the machine is comparatively new it may be worth contacting the maker direct or asking a local supplier if there is a maintenance service available so that the machine can be checked over and given a safety approval, if not a guarantee. If this is not possible check with a reliable professional, who may charge a fee to overhaul the

machine, but this will give you peace of mind that it is safe and worth the money and effort of installing it or using it in a re-designed kitchen.

Safety

The kitchen is a hazardous place with boiling water, pans of hot fat, toxic liquids, sharp knives and numerous opportunities for accidents to happen. During fitting and installation make sure than any risky or potentially unsafe area is made sound and place safety equipment, such as a fire extinguisher, in an area where it easily accessible and near the place where it may be needed.

If children have access to the kitchen, fit door fastening devices to prevent them from coming into contact with poisonous substances such as detergents or bleach. Put guard rails around hobs and

This page and opposite **This narrow, galley-style kitchen serves as a thoroughfare between two rooms. Since it opens directly onto the dining area, it needs to look elegant rather than wholly utilitarian. The pale wooden façades and steel sink and splashbacks contribute to its classic clean lines, and the unusual shelves with sliding door units are reminiscent of oriental screens. Ample storage means that utensils and cooking paraphernalia can be kept out of sight, leaving worktops clear. A hatch beside the hob gives easy access to the next-door room.**

Opposite **A Belfast sink is supported by a set of shelves. Pans are easily replaced after washing.** Below **Surfaces in a kitchen should be hygienic and easy to clean. Wood surfaces can be painted or sealed to make them resistant to water or, like this old table (left), covered in a thin sheet of steel.** Bottom **Overhead hanging storage is best kept to the middle of a work area so that you do not bang your head on the suspended pots and pans.**

cookers to prevent them from pulling pots and pans down on themselves. If possible fit a safety gate across the entrance to the kitchen so that younger children do not get underfoot or in the way.

Do not keep sharp knives in a cutlery drawer where you may cut yourself in the process of searching for them; have a specific wooden or plastic block placed in clear view on the work surface or a wall-mounted magnetic bar so that the knives can be kept together in an easily accessible place.

Within the kitchen there should be facilities to deal with an accident should one happen. For cuts and scalds a standard emergency medical kit, available from good pharmacists, should be on hand. For fires a fire blanket is useful, as is a hand-held extinguisher. Be sure that the extinguisher you buy is appropriate for its intended use, as some are formulated to deal with electrical fires and others with chemical combustion. If a localized fire does occur leave the pan or electrical item where it is; do not attempt to remove it until the fire has been put out and the item has had plenty of time to cool down. If it is electrical turn the power off at the mains before unplugging the appliance. Do not pour water on a burning pan of oil or fat as it may splash and cause burns. Note where the electrical mains cut-off point is, and the mains water tap, which you may need to turn off if the connection to a washing machine or tap disengages.

During the fitting stage make sure that you test machines as they are installed. If a cooker has a faulty valve or more serious problem it will be very difficult to remove once it has been secured in place and perhaps tiled around. Check the position and effectiveness of items such as extractor fans or vents – if they are too close to the hob the filters may become clogged with grease and in turn become a flammable source.

Once the installation is complete, take time before you sign any completion forms. Allow a few weeks to try, test and enjoy your new kitchen and equipment, and if during this 'honeymoon' period you find that something is chipped, scratched or damaged, call the company immediately. Although most firms have guarantees it may be harder to get them to come back and fix a problem when they have moved on to their next job or when months have elapsed, so make a close inspection as soon as you reasonably can.

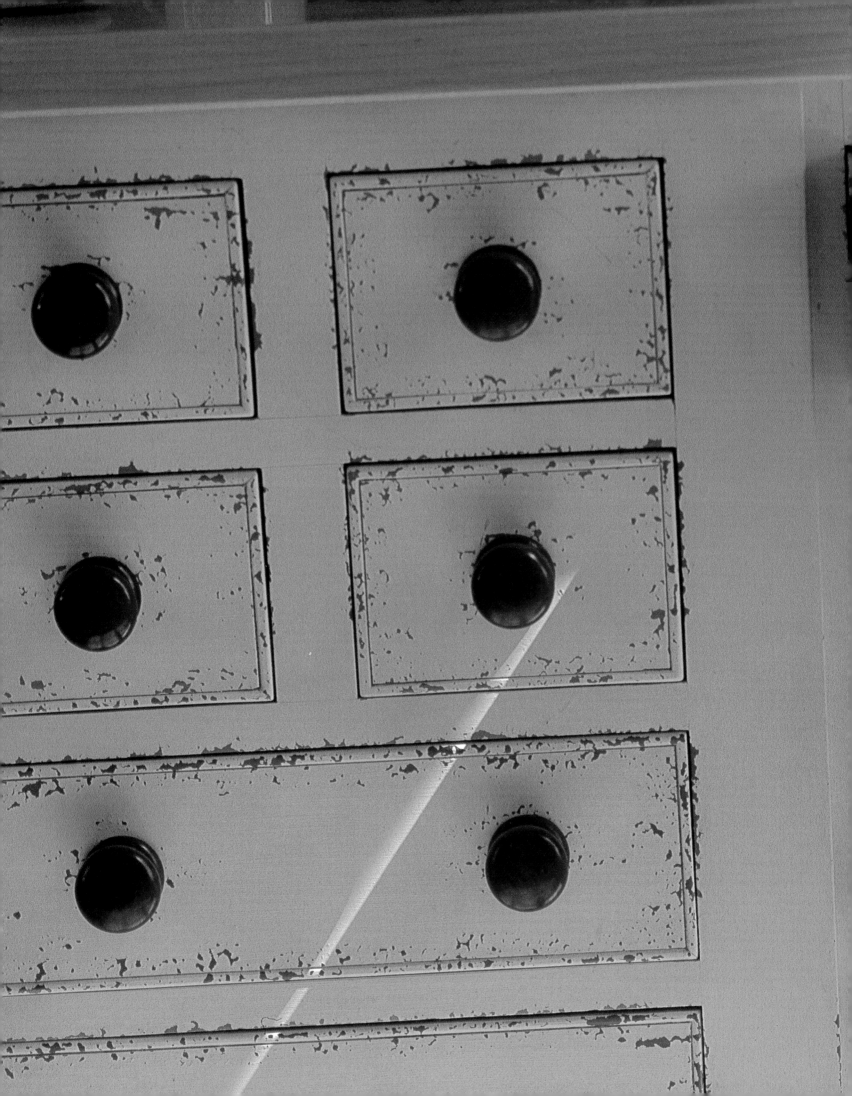

styles

traditional simple country

simple **modern** new professional

introduction

Choosing the overall style of your kitchen requires just as much thought and careful planning as the selection and siting of the major pieces of equipment. The appearance and design of the kitchen should be one you will be comfortable with on a day-to-day basis. There is no point in having decorations and furnishings in a style that will eventually prove to be boring or difficult to live with.

If you are basically a tidy person, then a full-blown rustic kitchen with open shelves, hanging plates and bunches of dried herbs may appeal in theory but irritate you when it actually comes to working there. Conversely, if you enjoy a relaxed approach to cooking and entertaining, you may eventually find the stark lines of a professional-style kitchen daunting. Also, beware of the fashionable fads portrayed in magazines. Just because a particular look may be in vogue, it does not mean it is practical for your home and lifestyle. Look at the reality of your situation – the photographs may show the Manhattan loft of a professional couple with no children who use the kitchen only to make coffee. If you live in a terraced house and have a young family, will the open shelves and etched glass of the kitchen in the magazine be durable enough? Are the white walls going to become marked quickly?

As well as your approach to cooking, take into consideration the setting of the kitchen. Look at the period and style of the whole room. Major structural features such as arches or unusually shaped windows or doorways might suggest a certain period or a style that is sympathetic to the surroundings. Equipment is also a factor. If you like retro-style machines such as 1950s refrigerators, these may suggest a certain look. But if the style of your machines and the decor you want do not correspond with each other, the problem can be overcome. Many large units can be camouflaged with a fascia to complement the rest of the units.

To help you decide on a style, consider collecting picture references and style pointers. Tear out photographs from magazines and illustrations from catalogues and brochures and gather swatches of colours, fabrics or surface materials that you like and stick them into a notebook. Jot down, in a few words or with a sketch, what you like and dislike about friends' kitchens. In a short while you will start to build up a visual reference as well as a practical list of dos and don'ts, all of which will help you when deciding on the style of your kitchen.

Opposite **While there are rules to planning and fitting a kitchen, the style of the fixtures and accessories is ultimately a personal choice.**

traditional
– a reassuringly
cosy and **homely**
environment

The Traditional style kitchen is perennial; for some people this look never goes out of fashion. The principles of its design are handed down from generation to generation, and are based on practical experience, accumulated through years of continuous adaptation and use. The basis of this style is essentially historic: it looks back to rural homes where the kitchen was not only the place where food was prepared and eaten, but it was also the main room where the family congregated, talked, drank and relaxed. This type of kitchen is based on the room that was truly the heart of the home.

There is inevitably a certain amount of nostalgic feeling connected with the Traditional kitchen – it is a reminder of times before high-speed modern life took over; it offers a reassuringly cosy and homely environment which can be understood and recognized by most people. But although the origins of the style may be basically quaint and old fashioned the look can be modified – it is a matter of personal taste as to which Traditional style you follow, and to what extent you adopt the look in terms of decoration.

Certain elements are important to achieve this look. Traditional kitchens can draw inspiration from local domestic sources, but they may also emulate decorative ideas found in other countries – places where the climate and way of life may seem attractive and appealing. For example, homes in cities as diverse as Leeds or Chicago may use decorative objects, tiles and colours that are from the countryside of Tuscany, Provence or Mexico.

Left **No other material suggests a traditional look as much as wood.** Far right **Unfitted units are most authentic for a traditional style kitchen but a mix of freestanding and fitted furniture can be used.** Right **Oil, gas or solid fuel ranges are often seen in this type of kitchen.** Below, left to right **The extractor hood has been disguised in a period style chimney canopy. Accessories are important; this old cutlery tray gives the right feel. Small round wooden knobs are appropriately simple. Classic panel detailing gives added interest to the doors.**

Right **With its high ceilings, this room is spacious enough to house a large arrangement of units along the end wall, designed to resemble an old-fahioned dresser. The dresser effect is achieved by placing a plate rack over the sink so that dishes, stacked after washing, provide a colourful and interesting focal point. Painting the top and bottom units in different colours gives the room an informal appearance and a less 'fitted' look. The panelled doors, small wooden knobs and pediment finish on the top of the upper cupboards and large cupboard to the right enhance the traditional image. To create a practical working area in this space an island unit is positioned between the sink and cooker areas, creating a basic work triangle. The dining table is placed to one side, clear of the working areas.**

Above **Old-fashioned brackets are used to support the plate rack and small metal hooks are ready to receive a row of cups or mugs. These sorts of small details are all important in achieving a well finished, traditional style kitchen.**
Right **In this type of setting a wooden draining board is appropriate – it complements wood used elsewhere in the furniture and has a classic, timeless appeal. It is specially treated to make it waterproof.**
Below **By simply rubbing or sanding the corners of drawers you can achieve a well-worn look.**

Opposite **This cooker is neatly fitted into a disused fireplace, allowing the chimney to be used as a conduit for the flue. The naturally irregular outline of the recess makes it an interesting feature and two small shelves provide dry, warm storage for herbs and spices.**
Far left **Enamel-fronted cookers are available in many colours, but choose a shade that will last through several changes in decoration: this type of cooker is an investment as well as heavy and difficult to install.**
Left **This unit has classic handles and a plain steel façade, which blend in with the eclectic mix of furniture.**
Below **Tailor-made to fit the space, this small end-of-worktop area is useful for resting dishes and utensils used during cooking.**

Whatever your reasons for choosing a traditional style of decor for your kitchen, your next step is to decide whether your theme is to be the full-blown old-fashioned look; a modern interpretation that dilutes the antiquarian feel with a careful selection of contemporary introductions; or somewhere in between these two extremes. Do you want a cacophony of colour with all the trimmings and accessories or just a subtle allusion to rural roots with a few well-chosen decorative pieces?

The original Traditional look has been updated by succeeding generations: the style has had to adapt to suit homes of vastly different architectural design, and to work around contemporary kitchen appliances that even those pursuing the most purist recreation of a period look would not do without. The open fire and blackened cast iron range have been replaced with solid fuel or gas stoves. Cold stores, larders and meat safes have given way to fridges and freezers and the bowl of well-drawn water to a sink and taps, and even that most 20th-century of inventions, the dishwasher. Although the overall look is reassuringly old fashioned, the technology, efficiency and hygiene standards are all bang up to date; traditional styling conceals the very best of contemporary labour-saving engineering.

For example, a kettle with an antiquated appearance but of current manufacture will be in keeping with the decor of the kitchen but offer modern competence. A row of stylish copper pans may be lined with the latest non-stick coating so that the outward show is conventional but in use they are efficient and effortless. Manufacturers cater for this taste, reviving the colouring, shapes and even packaging of designs from an earlier period. The New Maid whistling kettle is a prime example of this trend – a design from the 1950s with a Bakelite handle and spout and a rounded metalized body, it is once again a fashionable kitchen accessory. The Beam Balance scales, developed by F.J. Thornton in the 1900s are often

finishes, and worktops of wood or tiles. The splash-back could also be ceramic tiled or bare sealed plaster. A fitted Traditional kitchen can benefit from breaks and pauses in runs of units, which will create the effect of the kitchen being made up from a number of smaller units rather than one continuous line of cupboards fitted on all the walls. If possible try to vary the size of the units – put a double between two single units, then a double next to two singles – so that there is variation in the make-up rather than clumps of the same sized units above and below the work surface.

Some units can be left without solid doors. This device creates open shelving that is reminiscent of an old-fashioned dresser – the type of space where cookery books, letters, postcards, utensils and collections of old tins and boxes could be displayed. These showcase areas may have glass-fronted doors to keep

You do not have to sacrifice labour-saving appliances if you opt for a Traditonal-style kitchen – with clever planning they can be integrated without compromising the look.

seen in today's kitchenware suppliers and hardware departments. These typical Victorian scales with a cast-iron and brass base with a removeable brass dish and cast-iron weights are found in many kitchens, sometimes as a period-piece decoration but often as a fully functioning piece of equipment.

Traditional style kitchens can be fitted or free-standing. A fitted kitchen would offer a more contemporary interpretation of the look, with unit doors in solid wood, veneer or painted wood-effect

the items behind them clean and grease free. Plate racks can be fitted to hold everyday white crockery close at hand or a decorative display of a more prized collection of china.

The unfitted kitchen is more true to the original Traditional kitchen, which would have been an ad hoc collection of dressers, tables, cupboards and home-made shelves put together to create viable working and storage space. The most vital piece of furniture in the room would have been a large

Top left **Indispensible but unattractive modern appliances such as dishwashers can be concealed behind panels to match the other units.**
Top centre **Plain doors and classic handles lend stainless steel a timeless feel – simple styling can be 'dressed' or accessorized to suit most styles.**
Top right **A row of glazed tiles around the sink protects the wooden worktop from the worst of water splashes.**
Above **A plain white ceramic sink is the most classic choice.**
Opposite **The elements that give this kitchen a traditional or period feel are the extended plate rack and the brick shaped ceramic tiles.**

wooden table on which food was prepared and later eaten. The table was the main work surface and the focus point of the room. If you do not have the space to devote to a huge table the same effect can be created with an island unit in the centre of the room: it will offer the same combined working and dining space but also offer extra storage space in the cupboards below.

Large pieces of equipment, such as freezers can, if you want, be concealed behind cupboard doors or panels so that they blend in with the overall old-fashioned feel of the room, but items such as the cooker and sink, which will be permanently on show, should be chosen to be in

keeping with the look of the room. A white ceramic Belfast sink is suitable for most kitchens in this genre, but if you opt for a stainless steel sink it might be worth considering having it recessed beneath a wooden or polished stone work surface so that it is less conspicuous.

Colours and materials

Natural materials – historically the materials that were cheaply and readily available, such as wood, slate, stone, terracotta, rush and straw – are all appropriate, but they can all be used to create a contemporary look as an alternative to the more conventional age-old appearance.

Wood is ubiquitous: it is used for tables, chairs, cabinets, worktops, on floors and even as panelling on walls. Either varnished to reveal its inherent beauty and to protect its hardworking qualities, or painted in a variety of colours, wood is a vital ingredient in creating the Traditional look.

Far left **Tongue-and-groove panelling gives this room a timeless feel that is emphasized by unfitted furniture and open shelves.**
Left **A dresser has been made by placing an ornate cabinet under a row of shelves.**
Below, left to right **The classic curves of an Arne Jacobsen chair contrast with the parallel lines of the wall cladding. The recessed steel sink is modern but its simple shape sits happily in the mix-and-match style of the room. Wooden chopping boards create a pleasing arrangement.**

Accessories are an important part of the final dressing. This is not a clear surface kitchen, but one where the cook's tools are a feature of the display. Storage jars and utensils, crockery and glass, bottles of oil and bunches of lavender, garlic, chillies or herbs are used as decoration: visual stimuli to remind you of the purpose of the kitchen – a place to have fun, to cook, to dabble in the alchemy of mixing spices and flavours.

If the kitchen is also to be the place where you sit and relax, or chat with friends, then comfort should be the key word when choosing furnishings. Easy or armchairs, whether the fully upholstered version or a ladder-back chair with woven rush seat and arms, can be used. Harder wooden chairs should be softened with small decorative cushions which may be kept in place with ties or ribbons sewn to the corner and tied to the back legs or back uprights of the chair.

Floors can be wood, brick, terracotta tile or stone, scrubbed and waxed or sealed. To soften large expanses of floor, mats are often used. Woven straw or reed mats or cotton rag rugs are most authentic, but plain runners or dhurrie-style carpets can be effective.

If the setting is genuinely old there may be wooden beams in the ceiling, but if they do not exist you may want to add fake ones. If you do, make sure the wood you use is not too perfect – original beams are old, often gnarled and irregular although straight. Original beams would most likely have been hewn from a tree trunk by hand, using an adse or hand chisel; the indentations and imperfections add to the character. Also beware of staining the wood too dark: painting beams black can make them look Tudor rather than Traditional and they may appear as dominant black lines on a ceiling rather than an integral feature of the room.

Right, clockwise from top left **Glass-fronted cabinets provide light relief amongst rows of solid doors. An old beam acts as a backplate for utensil pegs. Sharp knives should be carefully stored; this recess keeps blades out of harm's way. Dried pulses and lengths of split bamboo have been used to fill the space behind the glazed panels of these drawers, creating highly original decorative drawer fronts. Pegs or hooks provide hanging space for utensils and tea towels.**
Opposite **Heavy old beams, such a feature of this room, lend themselves to traditional style.**

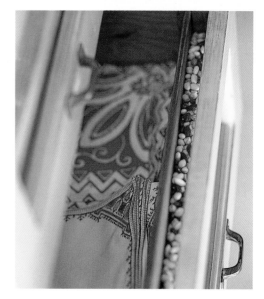

**simple country
- a classic
look updated**

Simple Country is less cluttered than Traditional style and, although based on old designs, it is has a more streamlined appearance and therefore a greater contemporary appeal. It is a style inspired by Northern European, Scandinavian and North American sources. The look is fresh, neat and uncluttered and, as in the Traditional style, units are made predominantly of wood, sometimes pale and plain but most often painted. In many ways it is a classic look, but it can be updated to make it more fashionable.

For example, the strength of colours used and the styles of accessories such as door knobs and catches that adorn the basic kitchen may change

from time to time. The design of the cabinets and furniture, however, is very much based on specific historic influences or an interpretation of a particular period or geographical region.

One of the strongest contenders of influence is Scandinavian style. This is essentially simple and uncluttered, with a liberal use of painted wood. Simple units, plate racks and dressers are all an integral part, although as with all historically based kitchens the units would originally have been free-standing and unfitted. For inspiration and decorative details look at the paintings of Carl Larsson, whose home at Sundorn in Sweden is where this light and airy and 19th-century style is

Opposite **The marble-topped table is reminiscent of French patisseries – it is also the ideal cool surface on which to roll out pastry for tarts.**
Above **Glass shelves provide light and visually pleasing storage space.**
Right **Glazed cupboards create an open and fresh feeling whereas solid doors might have created a darker and heavier feel.**
Top right **Fixed vertical dividers in extra-deep drawers create well-organized storage space for baking trays alongside the cooker.**

Left, top to bottom **This classic cooker suits all settings. Barley sugar spiral shelves make an interesting feature. An ornate wirework basket doubles as a glasses carrier.**
Opposite **A French café notice and decorative floor tile panels bring colour and style to this room.**

said to have been created. Other references may be found in Gustavian style, the slightly more elaborate and ornate decoration favoured at the time of King Gustav III.

Units in the Scandinavian kitchen may be edged, top and bottom, with simple carved pediments and pedestal details, making the units appear more as finished pieces of furniture rather than just storage units. Where shelves are left open for a display of china or bottles and jars of home preserves, they would be painted and edged with a length of scalloped-shaped cut paper or fine linen – but not too lacy or ornate. Units doors and dado or ceiling edge borders of simple, stencilled designs are also appropriate, in shades stronger than the general wall and unit, but still subtle and muted.

Not all unit doors need be solid: panels of fine chicken wire can be used, or finely pleated fabric. If the kitchen has a mix of freestanding and fitted units, a large cupboard, similar in size and proportion to a wardrobe, is a good Scandinavian feature. Again, the cupboard can be made to look lighter and less dominant by replacing the centre of the door panels with chicken wire or by stencilling a motif or monogram on it.

If fitted units doors are plain, you can create faux panels with painted lines to enhance the appearance and style of the room. To create the effect choose deeper shades of the base colour of the door – for example if the doors are painted a soft bluish

off-white, the faux panels can be created using a band of dark grey with a fine outer line of mid blue.

Small wall cabinets and painted shelves with decorated plinths are used not just for storage but also to decorate expanses of pale painted wall. These little chests and cupboards can have punched or cut wood patterns in them or be simply panelled with a few lengths of wooden beading.

One of the other most popular influences in this category is Shaker, inspired by the religious community who, in the early 1800s, settled around Maine and Kentucky in the northern regions of the United States of America. Two hundred years later the legacy of Shaker design and their practice of simple living is still admired, and although their original furniture designs have been adapted to suit modern materials, homes and lifestyles, the look has not changed that much. To emulate the look successfully it is useful to know a little about the people who created it and why they did so.

The principles of simplicity of design, crafts-manship and practicality were amongst the edicts of the Shaker movement, founded by Anne Lee who originally came from Manchester in England. In the communities there were many fine craftsmen and women who produced uncomplicated yet beautiful and functional furniture, boxes and baskets.

The Shaker motto was 'Hands to work and hearts to God' and they believed that the quality of their work, even in unseen places such as the back of a cupboard or the inside of a drawer, should always be of the highest standard because God is omnipresent and could see all. Quality is important in simple designs and furniture because there are no frills or fancy dressing to disguise inferior work-manship or clumsy finishes.

The Shakers also recycled furniture: if a bed was no longer needed it would be dismantled and the wood used to build something else that was required. The uncomplicated nature and quality of their work has made their furniture and style

Top left **A ceramic Belfast sink and a wooden draining board highlight the rustic feel.**
Far left **A kitchen table can be as basic as you like. This one is made from a box base with wide planks of mature wood laid across the top.**
Left **For protection from everyday wear and tear wood should be waxed or oiled.**
Opposite **Wood, wicker and earthenware pottery are all important ingredients of this style.**

Opposite **Old china and creamware are at home in the unfussy Simple Country kitchen.**
Far left **Instead of a row of solid overhead units a single glass-fronted display cabinet and a plate rack are more in keeping.**
Left **Kilner jars are useful air-tight storage for dried beans and pulses.**
Below left **Neatly arranged on shelves, even everyday plates and foodstuffs can be attractive.**
Below **A freestanding cabinet creates a focal point at the end of the room.**
Bottom **Old storage containers like this flour bin give an authentic touch.**

timeless and original. Antique Shaker furniture is now sought after and collected for contemporary as well as period homes.

Although some people may be fortunate to have antique or authentic furniture, modern copies and reproductions are generally of good quality, and it is a style that can be successfully recreated by a skilled carpenter or craftsman. Historically the kitchen would have been unfitted, made up of large cupboards and chests of drawers with a large scrubbed table, but in practical terms ordinary fitted units, simply grouped around the walls, can give you the modern version of the original style.

The basic kitchen should have simple, unfussy units, with a plain or tongue-and-groove effect centre panel and a broad relief border. To achieve a kitchen that emulates the authentic look all white goods such as fridges and freezers should be concealed behind faux doors or panels. It is not that the Shakers were against machines – in fact they were all for labour-saving devices, but the appearance of shiny contemporary pieces of equipment somehow detracts from the purity of the style. Door knobs should be plain and unfussy – round, plain polished or painted wood or white ceramic.

The peg rail, another Shaker trademark, is a band of wood with rounded wooden pegs inserted at regular intervals. The rail is a practical storage solution that can be used to hang pots and pans, kitchens linens such as aprons or towels, as well as jugs, mugs, sieves and ladles – in fact any kitchen gadget that has a handle and is not too heavy or bulky. In a small kitchen the rail may also be used to hang folding chairs from, keeping them

off the floor and providing valuable extra space in the centre of the room. The rails were also used to hang clothes and furniture from so that the floors could be easily and thoroughly brushed.

Colours and materials

The Simple Country kitchen is devoid of the clutter of traditional style. Herbs are not hung up to dry or on display, they are stored in neat containers on shelves. The mix and match collection of china is replaced by plain white plates and bowls or a collection from a matching dinner service in a low-key pattern. Colours tend to come from a limited palette and they are chosen to harmonize and co-ordinate rather than clash. It is altogether a more orderly look than Traditional style.

Top left **Corridors or lobbies can be used for overflow storage.**
Top right **A padded bench is comfortable enough for dining or relaxing.**
Above **Shelves across windows will give extra storage but allow light in.**
Opposite **The rafters and beams and an abundance of foliage add to the country feeling.**

Shaker kitchens tend to have white or cream walls with cranberry red, grey-blue or soft green painted units. Where natural wood is used it is often the warmer tones of cherry wood rather than the yellower tones of pine. As we know, Shakers were great recyclers so second-hand planks are ideal for flooring, doors or even worktops.

Continuing the theme of purity of style, the Shaker kitchen should be made of natural materials; shiny polymer finishes and an abundance of stainless steel would be out of place in this look. Although this style of kitchen may appear to be made from tongue-and-groove planking, the appearance can be deceptive. These days cabinet doors are often made from MDF which is routed and

grooved to make it appear as though it is genuine wooden planks. Once the MDF is painted it is very difficult to tell real wood from the substitute and MDF can be cheaper and more predictable (it is less likely to warp or bend than real wood).

Ceramic tiles are not generally a part of the Shaker kitchen brief, but where they are used in areas around a kitchen sink or as a splashback behind a cooker they are best left as simple as possible. No patterns or fancy borders should be used, just plain white or cream squares that will almost disappear into the wall colour. Hard natural stone materials, such as ornate or coloured marble or speckled granite, are other finishes that are not really appropriate to Simple Country kitchens.

Scandinavian colours tend to be pale washes of green, grey or blue. The fabrics and stencils can be brighter but they should not be too vibrant, although red, in conjuction with white, can be used sparingly. Gingham checked or striped patterns are popular, as are delicate sprigged or wildflower patterns, but do not try to add floribunda rose prints or Oriental bird designs – think about the floral and fauna native to Northern Europe; they will be the types of motifs appropriate on printed fabrics. Plain materials can be rich in texture: oatmeal and natural linens, hessian and jute, edged with borders of patterned fabric can be successfully used for cushions, covers and curtains. Embroidery and cut threadwork are also in keeping.

Tiles are more widely used in this kitchen and can be a mix of plain and decorative. Again, the patterns should be delicate and subtle, with maybe just a simple border and unobtrusive central design. These tiles should be smooth, unlike the rustic handmade ones favoured by Traditional style, and they should be thin, not thick and uneven.

Painted wooden floors are another feature of the Simple Country kitchen. A plain sanded floor can be edged with an uncomplicated border painted with dilute emulsion or watered down wood stain. The decoration can be kept simple or made more elaborate – to the degree where the pattern

The Simple Country kitchen combines old-fashioned comfort with a wealth of contemporary styling to create a warm and welcoming atmosphere.

assumes the colours and quality of a painted rug. Once the floor has been painted you can either leave it to age and fade under foot or seal it with a matt varnish which will make it more durable and help preserve the original strength of colour.

Another floor treatment that you may want to consider is bleaching wooden floorboards or liming them to achieve a lighter, weatherbeaten look. The pale tones achieved with these methods can look very attractive with the muted colours of the painted furniture and units and they can provide a good background on which to put brighter floor coverings such as rugs and mats.

Mats are sometimes seen in Shaker kitchens but these tend to be runners – strips of woven fabric – rather than generous rugs. In other Simple Country kitchens, homely rugs in colours to suit the scheme are both decorative and useful. If the other fabrics in the room are bright, say a rich blue and white check or a minty green and white design, the colours in the mat or rug could be chosen to co-ordinate or complement these.

Furniture and accessories are vital to complete the look. Chairs can be all wood or wood with wicker or woven straw seats. White or painted fine wicker can also be appropriate. The ladder back Shaker chair is another important feature that should be added to the kitchen if there is room. The chair is plain and unadorned, with a seat made of

woven cloth tape which is comfortable to sit on. Unlike the Amish, another religious community, the Shakers had a certain fondness for colour and modest decoration so the seats are often woven with different coloured warp and weft threads, creating a chequerboard pattern. The two tall upright back posts of the chair are finished with finials or pommels; these were not just decorative but were a practical and easy way to lift and move these lightweight chairs.

Accessories such as enamelware, punched metalware and simple bowls are often put on display in the Simple Country kitchen rather than hidden away in cupboards. Fine examples of needlework, such as simple samplers, can be framed and hung on the wall, and if a wall clock is to be added, it should be of painted and decorated wood as well. Other typical accessories include the distinctive oval Shaker storage boxes. Once used to hold flour, dried pulses and grain, these are now used for ornamental rather than functional purposes. Baskets were another popular storage container – they were originally hand woven from fine shavings of ash wood. Punch patterned metalware, such as candle sticks and wall sconces, can also be used to decorate.

Both the main styles of Simple Country can be used in old and more modern homes and the palette can be varied, within reason, to suit other interior schemes, but the essential ingredients are simplicity and a limited use of colour as well as abundant wood or wood effect materials.

This page, from top **Elements of Simple Country style include old-fashioned storage jars; fresh linen cloths, napkins and tea towels, and bringing the outside in, whether it is a bunch of wild flowers or a topiary in training.**

Opposite, clockwise from top left **An old-fashioned pot still makes excellent coffee. Bowls and dishes that do not match are fine. Pots and pans can be left on show. As long as it is clean and safe, faded and worn paintwork is acceptable. Open shelves are attractive but should be neatly arranged. Hanging racks come in many shapes and sizes. Keeping small items well stored and in order saves time. Authentic country sinks come in wood, copper or ceramic. Rows of gleamingly clean glassware are always a pleasing sight.**

simple modern
– streamlined
and uncluttered

The Simple Modern kitchen is a work place with a look that is pared down and neat yet not stark. It is easy to clean and maintain and can be quickly adapted to become part of a family breakfast room or a place for entertaining friends. Although primarily a practical space there is a certain softness in the fittings and decor which give it a homely and inviting feel. The overall style is mid-way between the high-tech austereness of the professional kitchen and the old-fashioned, conventional country look. Simple Modern is a design of kitchen that is increasingly popular and when planning or thinking about this look, bear in mind the old adage of 'Less is More'.

With their rationalized shape and uncluttered appearance, Simple Modern kitchens are ideally suited to small apartments or flats as well as metropolitan dwellings, but they can be adapted and enlarged to suit most settings. In properties where the back of the house has been extended to enlarge the kitchen, especially into a conservatory area or a wall with large sliding glass doors, this look can provide a link between old and new. As it has modern elements and it is not a dramatic statement of a definitive period it can rest easily in both the original and the new part of the room. With good planning the Simple Modern scheme can be a chameleon, blending and adapting to bridge the time gap.

Although the basic design principles follow the professional kitchen outline, being unfussy and streamlined, the colours and details come from the mellower spheres of country and Shaker inspired looks. The simplicity in its lines usually extends to having flat, almost featureless, door surfaces – no panels, beading or tongue-and-groove planks – with the exception of an unembellished handle or rail. This look can be achieved with totally fitted units or a mixture of free-standing and fitted. For example, base and overhead units could be installed to give a run of storage and worktop areas but expanded

Opposite **The hardness of metal can be softened with rounded corners.**
Top left **Clean, uncluttered lines are essential.**
Top right **The arched glass roof complements the adjoining building.**
Above left **A fine metal rod provides a practical hanging rail.**
Above right **Adjustable slat blinds can regulate the strength of light from the window.**

with the addition of freestanding elements, such as a tall cupboard or side-board, that match or contrast with the core kitchen. Although this style is best suited to a linear configuration, it is can be arranged and planned to work in more traditional formats.

The Simple Modern kitchen has to be carefully planned, with work areas, storage and work surfaces designed to cope with the demands of a smooth-running and efficient kitchen. Units are often built to accommodate the many machines and pieces of equipment that are an integral part of today's busy domestic life, such as fridges, freezers, dishwashers and washing machines, rather than leaving them on show. Larger appliances may be concealed behind faux panels or doors which match or co-ordinate with the rest of the units. Disguising or concealing large machines in this way has the effect of playing down the harder functional professional side of the room and promoting the softer, more decorative side.

This subtle change of emphasis can also be achieved with the introduction of softer unit shapes. Instead of the angular hardness of the professional kitchen this style tends to favour round and oval shapes. Cupboards with rounded corners help to create an easier appearance and are also more suit-able for a family to live with, as they are less likely to induce bruises when bumped against. This is not a totally uniform look so rounded shapes can be mixed with standard square or oblong units. Island units and peninsular bars may also double as breakfast benches or casual dining areas and the feeling is that the kitchen is integrated into the whole living area, rather than being a specific and isolated work place.

Most kitchens in this style will have one of the many domestic versions of the professional ranges used in restaurants that are now on the market, but some will opt for the wall-mounted double oven with one, if not both, being a convection oven. Some of the most recent designs of wall-mounted ovens have a flat computerized control panel which is operated by simply pressing the panel with a finger tip (there are no fiddly knobs or dials to collect grease or for a passer-by to knock against). The doors are often glass so that cooking in progress can be monitored, but the doors are so well insulated that little or no heat escapes and the door itself remains at room temperature. This type of oven also comes with a choice of a raised bar handle across the width of the door or a recessed handle that pops out when pressed.

Top right **A faux drawer front panel conceals an ingenious pull-out table.** Right **A marble inset in the wooden worktop next to the cooker provides a place to put down hot pots.** Opposite, clockwise from top left **The hardness of steel is softened with pale lacquered wood and a chequer-board slate floor. A few pieces of well-worn natural materials will alleviate the clinical overtones of high-tech machines and steel. Smart portable shelves hang from a peg rail. Classic, plain white china looks good in any style of kitchen.**

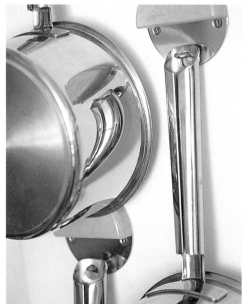

Instead of the large pantry-style combined fridge-freezer units, in this type of kitchen it is more usual to have a series of individual fridges and freezers that are fitted beneath the worktop. For example, there might be a standard fridge for daily use, a small freezer for easily accessible foods and a bottle fridge for wines, water and soft drinks. This configuration can be advantageous in smaller rooms or in a space that has a series of angles and corners that make it difficult to allocate the large area of wall and floor space that the bigger fridge-freezers require.

The few gadgets that are on display in the Simple Modern kitchen are selected design classics, such as the Phillipe Starck citrus press or the Dualit toaster, or the most modern Alessi kettle or coffee maker. Any old favourites that do not have the requisite appearance will be concealed in a cupboard and brought out only when they are to be used. Gadgets and accessories are specifically chosen to complement the colours and style of the kitchen: even the cookery books have designer status and there are no recipes on pages torn from magazines! In its most metropolitan and authentic interpretation this kitchen is a showcase as well as a serviceable location.

Utensils may be hung from a bar across the back of the worktop or on a panel next to the hob. Again, these items must be stylish; if the panel behind them is steel then the utensils should be steel, black or white. The modern ranges of spoons, tin-openers and peelers have attractive but very useful thick rubber hand grips. When these items are displayed on a rack they become a

Top left **Steel surfaces are durable but they may scratch; most should be cleaned with a soft cloth and a recommended cream cleaner.**

Top centre **Neat metal discs provide useful pot hangers and are positioned so that the top of the hanger protects the wall from the rim of the pot hanging above.**

Top right **The front of this unit has been softly curved, giving it a contemporary feel and a less rigid appearance.**

Above **A slim but useful cupboard has been fitted into a narrow gap.**

Above right **Instead of handles that stand proud these drawers are opened by recessed ovals.**

Right **Mixing unusual colours and matt and shiny surfaces gives a modern feel.**

Opposite **Using a combination of straight lines and curves gives this kitchen a fresh and interesting appearance. For safety, reinforced glass has been used to glaze the long curved windows.**

part of the decoration and a point of interest, so it is important that they are the sort of things you will enjoy looking at as well as using.

Lighting in this style of kitchen is often by halogen spot lights – small recessed ceiling lights that are directed to shine on the main work areas. Additional under-unit task lighting will also be necessary as this is a serious working kitchen and centre lights, if there are any, should be shaded with a classic chrome or a discreet unobtrusive shade, in keeping with the overall mood.

The Simple Modern kitchen has a broad appeal, with something to offer the single professional, a couple setting up home together or a growing family. It can be varied in severity to serve most tastes, from spartan and ascetic to simple and domesticated, without compromising the basic ingredients of the style. This category of design is a good starting point, a useful first kitchen – because the look is simple and understated it can be added to and adapted as needed. This look is something of a classic and although the machines may become outmoded and the accessories outdated, by changing the handles, taps and other details it can be updated without difficulty and with relatively little added expense.

Colours and materials

The decor and style of this kitchen should create the impression that the place is light and airy; if the room itself does not have these qualities they will have to be created. This can be done by putting skylights into the ceiling if the kitchen is directly under the roof, or by opening up a side wall to create a bigger window or french doors. If light cannot be brought into the room by structural alterations then the effect must be artificially created with the use of colour and cleverly positioned lighting.

It is appropriate then that the colours and materials of the Simple Modern kitchen are from a palette that is bright and light. Colours tend to come from the paler side of the spectrum, a wash or hint of colour rather than a rich or jewel shade, though a more random effect of units in mixed paintbox colours can also look good. White is a universally popular colour for kitchens and it is particularly suited to this look, but it

Opposite **Utilitarian corrugated steel creates an interesting undulating cladding for the splashback and island unit.**
Top left **Carousel pot shelves swing out from a deep cupboard and are useful in corner units.**
Top centre **Smooth sheet steel has been used to create water-tight joints around the sink.**
Above left **Steel also makes a hardwearing wall covering, resilient to kicks and knocks.**
Above centre **A traditional waste bin complements the corrugated walls.**
Above **Bright colours zing out against the steely grey background.**

is mixed with other colours and textures to prevent the look from becoming too clinical or bland. Dilute citrus shades such as yellow and green can be used successfully, as can naturally inspired tones such as oatmeal and khaki. These pale colours may be edged or contrasted with a darker version of the same shade or with pure white.

A very interesting effect can be created by using pale coloured units with stainless steel splashbacks and kickboards. Add a polished grey or black granite or slate worktop to this muted scheme and the dark band of the worktop immediately draws the eye to it and it can create the illusion that it floats against the pale background. This can lend a stylishly dramatic touch to an otherwise understated kitchen.

Materials appropriate to a Simple Modern kitchen include the harder surfaces of steel, chrome, granite, marble and glass, but these can be softened by complementing them with wood. Wood can remain natural or be painted, but the timbers chosen are usually pale ones such as beech or maple or warm shades of cherry or rosewood, rather than the darker types, such as mahogany or stained oak, which are best used for period or country styles.

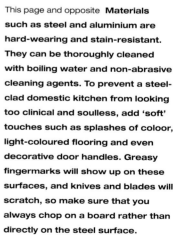

This page and opposite **Materials such as steel and aluminium are hard-wearing and stain-resistant. They can be thoroughly cleaned with boiling water and non-abrasive cleaning agents. To prevent a steel-clad domestic kitchen from looking too clinical and soulless, add 'soft' touches such as splashes of coloor, light-coloured flooring and even decorative door handles. Greasy fingermarks will show up on these surfaces, and knives and blades will scratch, so make sure that you always chop on a board rather than directly on the steel surface.**

Glass is widely used in this category of kitchen. Strengthened glass – plain, opaque or patterned – can provide light relief from solid MDF or steel panel doors. Glass doors or inset panels also add a less formal and business-like finish as well as making it easier to see what is in the cupboards, while keeping grease and dust off the objects inside. Glass is best used in upper wall-mounted cupboards where it is less likely to be smashed, and also where light makes it easier to see into the cupboards, but if a specially toughened safety grade is used to prevent accidents, glass can make an interesting display feature out of a row of floor units.

Manmade materials such as coloured laminates and resin finishes are also popular. These new laminates come in a spectrum of bright colours and may have patterns or designs as an integral feature. In combination with plain surfaces they can be used to achieve a lively but not overpowering scheme. They are durable and easy to wipe clean, as well as requiring little or no maintenance. Practical considerations such as these are well worth contemplating because this style of room is best kept neat and tidy. Clutter, scuffs and smears will look out of place and detract from the overall appearance.

Units doors should be a single plain colour with practical but stylish handles or bars. The pale background will make the handles stand out as a feature so it is worth investing a little time and money to locate good-looking, quality door furniture. Handles, railings and bars work best when they are plain and unadorned in design. Steel is an excellent choice, as is brass, which has a warmer, more mellow appearance.

Left **One-room living – the kitchen, dining and seating areas are all together. The steel trim in the kitchen is echoed in the chrome frames on the chairs and sofa. The use of the same flooring throughout gives a feeling of unity, but the long row of units forms a definite divide.**
Above left **Storage on display should be neat and uniform.**
Above right **The sink is slightly lower than the worktop so that a low splashback keeps spray in check.**

Top **When choosing handles for drawers and doors try them out to see if they suit your grip and hand size. Also remember that handles may need to be cleaned if grabbed by flour-covered or greasy hands, so avoid anything too fussy or ornate. Where you position the handles is also important. On upper cabinets you should place the handles on a lower edge so that they are within easy reach, and on lower cabinets position them so that you do not bump against them as you are standing at the counter.**

Above **Space within drawers may need to be sub-divided to contain smaller items.**

Above right **Long door handles mirror the uprights of the staircase in this modern interior.**

On top of the plain units there should be a long clean length of worktop interrupted only by an inserted appliance such as a hob or sink that cannot be concealed. The wall adjoining the worktop is another area where a plain and durable surface should be placed, but it may be in a contrasting material and colour to the units and worktop. This splashback area is often punctuated by a narrow gadget rail from which small shelves, utensils and kitchen towel holders may be hung.

Ceramic tiles are found in the Simple Modern kitchen but they are often matt rather than highly glazed, and for splashback areas they tend to be

small mosaic-sized squares. Shiny surfaces are restricted to the muted sheen of stainless steel and the polish of a chrome rail – highly glazed tiles can look brash and cheap in this minimalist setting. Ceramic colours are usually kept pale and light with little or no decoration as these tiled areas are not designed to draw attention. They are functional rather than decorative and should blend in with the wall or unit colour.

By contrasting textures and colours in a scheme you can bring interest and variety without having to resort to overblown patterns. Black-and-white checkerboard tiles may be used in some cases, but apart from a sharply graphic design such as this Simple Modern is not a look that works well with floral patterns or ornate designs on surfaces or soft furnishing fabrics.

Floor surfaces can be of wood, linoleum or tiles and old floorboards will blend with any colour scheme and provide a neutral base for even the more high-tech styles of Simple Modern designs. Again matt finishes are preferable to shiny ones (shiny floor surfaces are to avoided in kitchens generally as they can become dangerously slippery if water or another liquid is spilled on them).

Floor surfaces are best left bare, not dotted with mats or rugs, which belong elsewhere in other kitchen styles. Even if the room is a kitchen/dining or kitchen/family area the overall appearance should be unadulterated and fresh. Floor areas can be defined by changing the colour and shape of the floor covering itself, to help differentiate between two functions. For example, the floor area of the kitchen could be laid with a pale, dove-grey linoleum which curves majestically to the outer edge of the end of the peripheral unit. On the far side of this curve, covering the area designated to be the dining room, the tone of the linoleum could change to a deeper charcoal shade.

If you are using wood flooring in a large room that contains two functions, or two smaller rooms have been knocked through to make one, keep the grain and direction of the floorboards in a continuous through line. This will help to give a feeling of length and perspective to the room. If you are laying a new floor, wide planks will achieve a more contemporary look than the traditional narrow boards. There will also be fewer boards to lay down.

Right **When you are deciding which oven or hob you might have in a new kitchen remember to think in practical terms as well as considering how different models would fit in with your chosen style of decoration. Look at the cooking equipment you already have and check whether it will still be suitable for use on a different sort of cooker. For example, if you have had an Aga or a traditional range the more robust cookware, pots and pans that are suitable for that type of use may not be the right thing for a modern halogen hob. To get the best results from your hob and cooker it is important to have the right equipment to suit the heat source and type of cooking you favour, so be prepared for extra expenditure if you do need to completely replace your *batterie de cuisine*.**

new
professional
–a practical
and utilitarian
appearance

Opposite **Practical but not dull, the New Professional kitchen is for the keen cook.**

Top left **For a uniform appearance machines such as dishwashers should be clad with a fascia that matches the other units.**

Top right **An integral worktop and sink has completely smooth lines.**

Above left **Long handles enable the drawer to be opened easily from either side.**

Above right **Steel surfaces can be sterilized with boiling water.**

Right **Reinforced safety glass is a welcome addition in contemporary kitchen design.**

The New Professional kitchen gained enormously in popularity in the late 1980s and early 1990s. Today it is one of the most desirable choices of new kitchen design, particularly for people planning a new kitchen from scratch (it is not a look that works successfully with a mixture of old and new fittings, so it is best to start over anew if you are planning on creating this type of kitchen). Inspired by commercial equipment and locations, the defining feature of this style is its businesslike and functional nature. The sort of cooking, refrigeration and ventilation units that were originally intended for use in restaurants and hotels came into the home, and started the trend for unfussy, clear-cut, serious cooks' kitchens.

The interest in professional catering equipment came about through two channels. Firstly there was an appreciation of the clean, uncluttered lines and large capacity of the apparatus and its easy-to-maintain silvery metal casing. Secondly came the influence of food fashion, and the trend toward grilled, griddled and charcoal-seared foods such as vegetables, fish, chicken and other meats. The conventional ovens that were available for the domestic market could not produce the same effect as the high-temperature eye-level grills or the charcoal effect griddles that were available on the commercial machines.

Many owners of converted loft and warehouse apartments, where space was not a problem, installed the true professional multi-oven, with extensive grills and six to eight gas rings, large 'walk-in' fridges and steel food preparation areas. The New Professional look is best suited to open-plan living as the commercial size large scale equipment requires more floor and height space, and a small galley or cottage kitchen would be overwhelmed by the purists' choice of professional equipment. In time, domestic manufacturers picked up on this trend and they started to produce commercial type ranges of equipment for the home. These ranges were adapted to suit smaller kitchens and lay cooks who were intending to feed a family and friends rather than a restaurant full of clients. The new style ranges were also more suited to the home, because the high heat output and excessive energy consumption of the commercial ranges were moderated and reduced, and extra safety features were incorporated.

Opposite **The high back on this unit conceals the work area of the kitchen from the living area.**
Far left **The hob is surrounded by metal casing to match the units.**
Left **Wooden flooring gives a softer, more domestic touch to the professional style equipment.**
Below left **A wall of sliding glass panels protect the shelves from the grime and grease of the kitchen.**

With these types of cooker the single basic unit stands alone but it can be added to. For example, a plate warmer unit may be installed to the side of the cooker to keep plates and cooked foods warm and an eye-level grill can be fixed above the hob area or over the built-in charcoal grill range, another additional feature. Therefore it is easier to customize this type of cooker to suit your own individual needs and requirements.

Fridge-freezer manufacturers were also quick to respond to the swing of interest towards the larger machines. Although it has been very popular in North America for many years, the ice-making, 500 litre (100 gallon) capacity larder fridge was a comparitive rarity in the UK and most of Europe.

Inspired by the cult of the celebrity chef and by the large-scale commercial equipment found in restaurant kitchens, the New Professional kitchen has been adapted for the domestic environment by serious cooks, and there is no compromise on function or form.

But American manufacturers started to export their fridge-freezers from the US to meet the demand, and in order to compete, European manufacturers soon increased the size and altered the styling of a number of their machines.

When a kitchen is fitted with these larger, more powerful appliances, it is advisable to follow the whole system through and install an effective, full-size, professional extractor fan to remove cooking smells, grease heat and moisture. An open-plan living area will not have the divisions or walls to contain steam and odours so an effective extractor is important. Also in terms of size and proportion, if you fit one large unit, such as a cooker, for the overall balance and appearance of the room the other machines and units should be of a similar generous scale.

If you do not have the luxury of a huge open-plan loft in which to install a full-scale New Professional kitchen, but you are nevertheless determined to create the look in your home, you could compromise by selecting appliances that are designed for the domestic market but suggest the serious look. Standard 90 cm (36 in) wide gas ranges, or dual fuel ranges with gas powered burners and self-cleaning electric ovens, can give the effect and appearance of a commercial cooker but at a scaled-down size. Even some of the more conventional fridge-freezers can be ordered with silver or charcoal grey finishes instead of the traditional white, or custom clad in fine steel sheeting, all of which give the clean cut, industrial look that is the essence of the professional style.

It may not seem apparent at first from the streamlined effect but the New Professional kitchen can be freestanding. Although they are heavy, many of the commercial-style ranges can be installed and fitted to electricity and gas, but when it is time to move on the connections can be turned off and (admittedly with the help of several strong helpers) the cooker may be moved. A freestanding stainless steel fridge-freezer, with the regulation steel casing, is also a moveable feast. Utilitarian metal or Dexion shelving may be used to provide storage space for dried and tinned foods as well as china, cutlery and pots and pans. This can easily be dismantled and re-assembled in a different location. Industrial-supply perforated aluminium baskets stacked on a central pivot or arranged on a sliding shelf system, as well as metal grid hanging racks, can also be taken apart and moved. Sinks and extractor hoods, with all their mains plumbing, ducting and waste pipe connections, may be a little more difficult to remove, but the majority of the units and appliances of the kitchen are readily dismantled and removed.

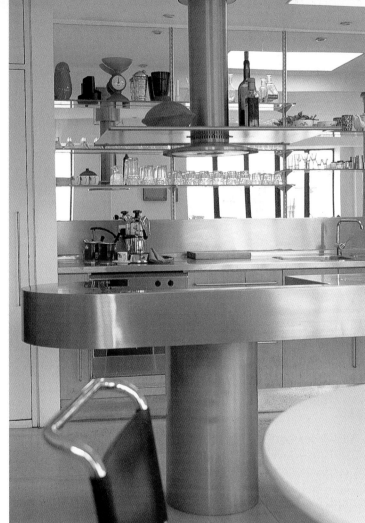

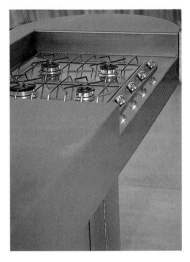

Top left **The support pillar is also a small cupboard.**
Top right **A mirrored wall reflects daylight back into the room.**
Above left **The recessed hob is invisible from elsewhere in the room.**
Above **Long handles are less likely to cause bruises than round knobs.**
Opposite **Two lengths of worktop create a galley style kitchen. Rounded edges soften what might otherwise be an austere layout.**

Sinks are usually moulded as an integral part of the work surface on either side of them. The sink is formed in a long sheet of steel, the sides of which become the work surfaces. This single moulded sheet eliminates joins and recesses around the sink where bits of food or dirt might lodge, and because the surface is continuous, it is easier and more efficient to clean. However, it is advisable to use a specific smooth, cream cleaning agent for these surfaces as many standard products contain tiny particles of abrasive which may scratch and damage the polished steel. Where steel is not used as a work surface, a self-contained laboratory sink may be fitted between worktops, or a smaller steel sink may be recessed beneath a thick surface of terrazzo, granite or marble, in a steel-like or darker grey colouring. These are all practical, easy to clean and hardwearing surfaces.

Colours and materials

In minimalist kitchens the choice of materials is crucial, because it is they that create the colour, texture and form rather than peripheral objects such as accessories, pictures or fabrics. Although the main pieces of equipment, such as the cooker, fridge-freezer and dishwasher, might have been adapted and evolved to suit domestic use, the basic professional look and style of the kitchen remains, so it follows that the decoration should, strictly speaking, be clinical, with white walls and tiles and steel worktops, sinks and unit doors, but in domestic settings colours have crept in.

At first the stark white of the true professional setting was softened with neutral and natural stone and putty colours, then pastel shades were used to soften the hard appearance of the steel units and brushed aluminium trim.

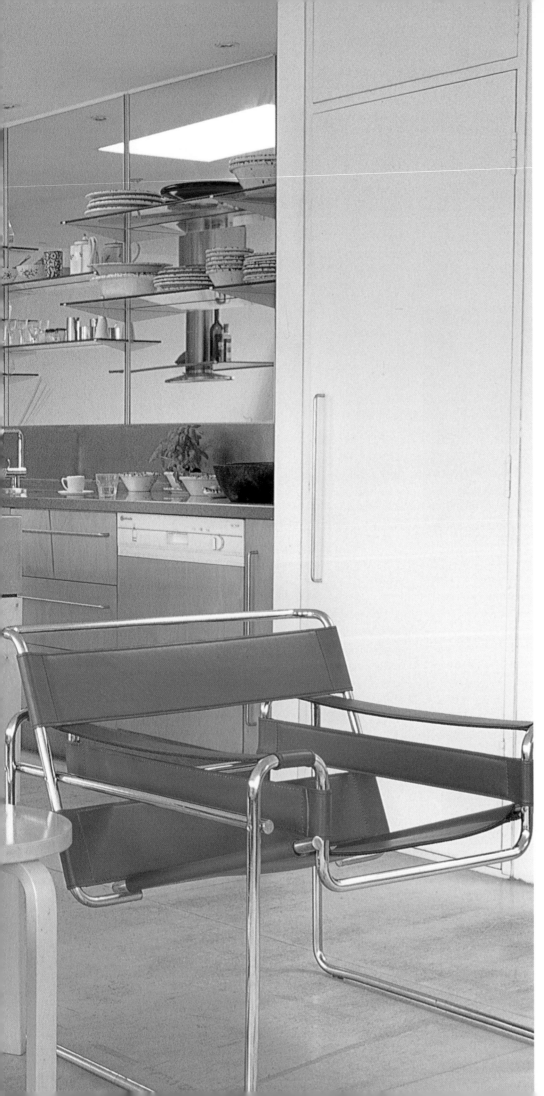

Moving on from these muted shades some of the more adventurous designers started to add single, strong colours, such as a rich deep blue, acid green or strong buttermilk yellow for a wall of tall units, a single area of splashback or a length of worktop. The use of a single area of vivid colour such as this created an attention grabbing highlight in the otherwise monotone surroundings. Other compromises that have occurred as the look became established include the use of opaque reinforced glass for door panels instead of steel or brushed aluminium, which again serves to lighten the overall appearance. The splashback area behind the worktop and sink, in both the professional and the adapted professional kitchen, are predominately steel, although reinforced opaque glass panels are again used to give a lighter appearance. Sometimes polished black granite or sealed slate is used, but this tends to give a harder and darker appearance to the scheme.

In a real professional kitchen, the utensils and storage jars would be kept off the work surfaces and stored in pantries and the outer work areas of a hotel or restaurant kitchen. In practice, these

Left **The New Professional kitchen is low key in colour and embellishment so any other furniture in the room will stand out against this neutral background. These classic seats by Charles Eames, Alvar Aalto and Marcel Breuer are perfect in this type of setting.**
Above **A deep steel skirting board brings the metal of the worktop and the splashback to floor level, giving a finished look to the scheme.**

Top row, left to right **Thick glass tiles conceal built-in lighting. The use of steel extends to the utensils. Wooden chairs and a round table soften the hard-edged kitchen. Steel surfaces reflect available light. A steel-fronted cooker fits perfectly.** Bottom row, left to right **A gleaming surface always looks good. Marble and stone are compatible with steel.**

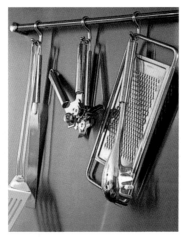

items tend to find their way back into the domestic kitchen but, in the spirit of the style, storage jars tend to be matching sets, rather than an eclectic hotch-potch, and in utilitarian materials and shapes. Utensils, again mainly made from aluminium, chrome or steel, in uniform style, are hung from business-like metal rails or wire mesh racks.

Although the overall features and styling of the New Professional kitchen are futuristic and modern, the flooring is often made from more conventional materials. In lofts, warehouse apartments or other homes where wood flooring exists this often remains, although it may be sanded to give a clean, fresh

Gleaming uncluttered surfaces reflecting light-filled interiors, sleek architectural lines and state-of-the-art appliances and gadgets – all are the hallmarks of a New Professional kitchen.

appearance and sealed with a matt varnish instead of a stained or high gloss finish. Pale sandstone or slate tiles complement the look well, as does sealed MDF, industrial linoleum and rubber flooring or epoxy resin coated concrete.

As light is important in all kitchens, but especially this one, windows should be minimally clad with plain roller blinds or shutters that can be folded back into a small space when not required. Hanging fabric curtains will only become soggy, steam damaged and stained, so it is best to leave them for a living area. If the room is overlooked so that privacy becomes an issue, you

might consider putting opaque glass in the lower half of a window, leaving the top in clear glass to allow in maximum light and to create a feeling of space. Artificial lights can be recessed into the ceiling or under wall cabinets and directed so that they illuminate worktops and cooking areas, but with highly reflective surfaces like steel, chrome and aluminium in abundance you have to be careful that you angle the lights to avoid glare and flare. Halogen spot lamps are the ideal choice.

As this style of kitchen tends to be linear, with the cabinets and machines fitted along one main wall or divided between opposite or adjoining walls, the straight, parallel lines of the layout are often emphasized by the use of full length chrome, satin nickel or polished steel handles on the units. These handles stretch across the width of a cupboard door or unit and are practical because you can grab them and pull the door open at any point along the handle, rather than having to grip a specific small knob in the centre of the outer edge of the door. Fittings such as handles tend to be chosen for their simple style and practical qualities rather than pretty styling.

These qualities also apply to the choice of tap. In many cases industrial lever taps are chosen because they are easier to turn on and off with the elbow when hands are greasy or covered in dough or flour. But for the very reason that they are easy to turn on and off, such taps can be wasteful of water, and so they may not conform to building regulations for domestic use, so check with your local authority before you have them fitted. Single spout mixer taps are always popular, here because of their minimalist appearance, but also because they supply the right temperature of water from one nozzle, avoiding the need to fill up a sink with hot and cold water until you achieve the right mix.

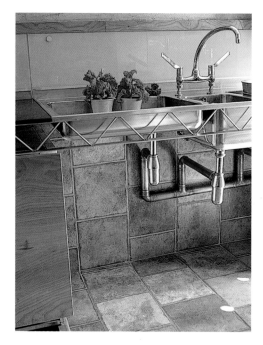

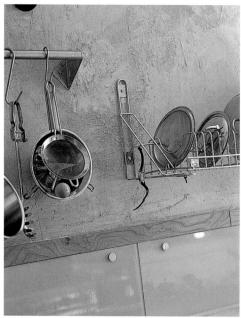

Other practical considerations include the location of plug sockets. These are usually located along the wall nearest the worksurface where electrical appliances might be used. In the New Professional kitchen they may be concealed beneath the edge of an island or peninsula work station, or grouped in blocks and covered with a protective shield which can be flipped up to give access to the sockets. Light switches may also be covered in a silvery steel-effect casing so that they are in keeping with the rest of the surface area.

When it comes to adding furniture such as tables and chairs to this style of kitchen you are in fact deviating from the original plan – in a professional kitchen there simply would not be a dining area. The chef may have a small dining table in his office where he can entertain guests, but essentially the professional kitchen is a working area, a place of frenzied activity where there is no time to sit around relaxing and sipping coffee.

If a peninsula or island unit is in the plan then streamlined stools with silvery chrome or steel-like legs would be in keeping, but as with the floors which may be traditional or old wood, the furniture most often used in this style of kitchen is not necessarily high-tech or avant garde. Arne Jacobsen 'Ant' chairs with their distinctive rounded back and seat are ubiquitous, even though they were

designed and originally produced in the 1950s. Aluminium Push Boy bins with the flip tops are also retro style but are suitable for this modern look.

When buying china, glass and cutlery suitable for this kitchen, think workmanlike and practical. Plain white china, unfussy cutlery and simple, clear glass are the ideal (in many hotels and restaurants plain white china is used to concentrate attention on the food rather than the fancy rim of the plate). It is also easier to replace a broken white plate than to find the exact match for a coloured or patterned version. You can also mix various styles and types of white plates – because they are all the same colour the table setting has a unity.

Opposite page, clockwise from top left
Maximum exposure is part of the New Professional style: working parts such as pipes and ducts may be left on show if they look good. A triangular metal bracket on the worktop breaks up the parallel lines. Racks and rails for storage ensure everything is easy to reach.
This page, clockwise from top left **Sleek featureless units marry well with the regular lines of the rest of the kitchen. A well-planned run of units fills a compact space. Professional style equipment has been scaled down for domestic use.**

equ

ipment

lighting **surfaces** plumbing
appliances accessories
cabinets furniture **display**

introduction

Once you have decided on the structural layout and style of your kitchen it is time to examine the details such as the finish for doors, floors, work surfaces and splashbacks, as well as the equipment, both large and small. There is a bewildering assortment of choices in each category, so it is wise to set a price limit and be sure of your requirements before you make a commitment or go out to buy.

Before the units and work surfaces are installed work out your lighting plan, so that the wiring and fittings, which may need to be recessed into the ceiling, can be put in place. With surfaces, the choice can be narrowed down to those materials that are suitable for the style and colour range of kitchen you have chosen. Price may play a part in your choice: some finishes are attractive but expensive, and a cheaper alternative may be found that creates a similar look but is still within your budget. You may also be influenced by the number of years you plan to live in your home.

When you are choosing equipment, spend time visiting showrooms and reading magazines and manufacturers' literature about the latest technology and gadgets. Advances in engineering and energy-saving devices have come a long way in recent years. Whereas you might once have bought a microwave oven that cooked but did not brown, now there are machines that can do both. But even the mighty microwave may disappear in time, as the facilities it provides are incorporated into regular cooking structures. Among the latest machines are those that combine the cooking abilities of gas with the microwave's speed, reducing conventional cooking time by 50 per cent.

Developments in environmental areas of design and production are having a decisive influence and will continue to do so. There are eco cycles in washing machines and dishwashers that can be used for smaller and light-stain loads, saving water and electricity. The market for single household equipment has also grown, with demographic profiles showing that more people live alone. Manufacturers now supply machines to meet these requirements and are becoming increasingly open to tailoring or creating designs to more individual requirements.

So when embarking on the difficult task of buying equipment, be sure in your own mind what it is you want the machines to do, but have an open mind as you may find that where there used to be a number of separate machines to perform a variety of tasks, there is now one gadget that combines two or three operations in one.

Opposite **Once the skeleton of your kitchen is in place it is time to fill it with all your favourite gadgets and tools.**

lighting

Lighting is a complex topic but one that is very important in a kitchen. It is best planned in conjunction with a professional, and it should also be fitted by a qualified electrician. Most people want light sunny kitchens but due to location or the direction in which the windows face it is not always possible. To create the sunny look, as well as a safe and efficient kitchen, artificial lighting should be carefully chosen and well installed.

As well as achieving the right ambience for the room, lighting is vitally important for safety reasons – to illuminate surfaces where you will be using sharp knives, and where there are hot rings or ovens. Storage areas should also be efficiently lit, whether by individual, fluorescent mini-strips activated as the door is opened or by spotlights fixed above.

Lighting is divided into two main areas: ambient and task. Ambient light is what is used to illuminate the whole room. It should ideally be on a dimmer system so it can be adjusted to suit the required mood. The main lighting may be provided by a cluster of recessed spotlights, supplemented, if necessary, by a pendant or feature light over a table area.

A hanging light has an aesthetic and a functional role in that it helps to break up the mass of horizontal lines created by rows of units, and may also make a high ceiling appear lower. Some pendant lights come with variable-height mechanisms,

Opposite **Louvered blinds can be adjusted to direct the angle and amount of light.**
Right **Two large inset windows bring daylight into this kitchen and a candelabra offers a more romantic form of lighting for the evening. Another hanging light provides an electrical alternative, useful on dark winter mornings or dull afternoons when candlelight would be out of place.**

Above **Electric striplights can be installed under units to focus on the worktop areas where food is prepared. The pale flooring and unit fronts, along with the white splashbacks and ceiling, help to make the make the room feel light and airy.**
Above right **This wall-mounted adjustable light can be shone directly onto the work surface as a task light; alternatively, it can be angled so that the light is shone up the wall. The latter option is ideal for evening dining in the kitchen because the diffused light is softer and more relaxing than direct light.**
Opposite **These oversized industrial light shades are a prominent feature of the otherwise plainly decorated kitchen.**

which mean they can be pulled down low over the table for intimate suppers or raised for other meals and table top activities.

Task lighting, which is light targeted at specific work areas, can be created with small fluorescent strips, a low voltage mini halogen fixture or strips of tiny bulbs in a rubberized casing, like Christmas tree lights in a transparent garden hose. The latter offers edge-to-edge lighting under a cupboard and a soft but clear overall span rather than a specific or directed spot of light. Task lighting should be positioned at the front edge of upper cabinets,

rather than to the back, because bulbs placed at the back of the unit will illuminate the splashback rather than the worktop area where the activity is taking place. The correct positioning is important as badly positioned lights will cause your hands, and in some cases your body, to cast shadows over the task you are performing, hindering your view and consequently your safety.

Other areas where task lights will be useful include the sink and hob. Hob lights may be fitted under the extractor hood, if there is one; if not they could be recessed into the ceiling above or suspended from a gantry and pointed at the hob. The light from these overhead fittings may be directed more specifically by using a baffle or shield so that there is a direct beam rather than an amorphous pool of light. At the sink both the bowl and the draining board should be lit. This may not at first seem necessary if the sink is in front of bright sunny windows, but at night or on dark winter's afternoon, the artificial light will compensate for the lack of natural light, making it easier to ensure that dishes are clean and that boiling water or the contents of draining pans hit their target.

If you have high gloss resin or stainless steel surfaces be careful that lights do not cause glare – this can be controlled and minimized if the bulbs have a frosted or opaque finish. Other worktop and splashback materials such as dark shades of

granite or slate will absorb a lot of light, as will dark wood cabinets, so more lights or bulbs with increased power may be necessary.

Types of light

There are three main types of light available: halogen, which is a very clear white light; tungsten or incandescent, which is the softer yellow light that most of us know; and the very bright and powerful fluorescent. Ideally you should use more than one type of bulb to light the kitchen. A mix of halogen and tungsten light can create a good overall effect.

Left **The utilitarian appearance of this adjustable wall-mounted light is in keeping with the steel worktops and functional hanging rack.**
Above **A clip-on light will provide illumination in areas where a socket is not directly available.**
Opposite, left, from top **A row of small sealed lights can be used instead of a conventional striplight. Pendant lights are attractive but should not be used above hobs or ranges, where heat may damage cables. A scissor mechanism allows the light to be pushed neatly back to the wall.**
Opposite, right **Decorative ceramic shades and containers introduce a retro feel to this dining area.**

Incandescent lights are fine for general room lighting but you can do better for task lighting. Halogen bulbs are generally very small and fragile, and should not be touched directly since grease from the skin may damage the bulb – always hold new halogen bulbs in a clean cotton cloth when placing them into sockets. The bulbs are often tiny, so they are unobtrusive and very suitable for recessed ceiling lights. They last longer than tungsten so they do not need to be replaced so often, a bonus when the light fitting is inaccessible. The light emitted by a halogen bulb is clear, bright and white but the bulb itself can become very hot, so do not install it at lower levels or in areas where a hand or arm may come in contact with it. If a clear halogen bulb is too bright, try a frosted type, which will give a more diffuse and less glaring beam.

Tungsten or incandescent bulbs give a yellow hue and the output of light can be varied by using a dimmer switch. This type of lighting is not good for food preparation areas but it has a softness that makes it ideal for the dining and relaxing areas of the room. Tungsten bulbs have a shorter lifespan than fluorescent or halogen bulbs and can become warm to the touch.

Fluorescent strips were popular in the 1960s and 1970s, but the blue, bright lights have come a long way since then. Fluorescent tubes can now be bought with the equivalent light and colour as day light. Fluorescents are also energy efficient, lasting

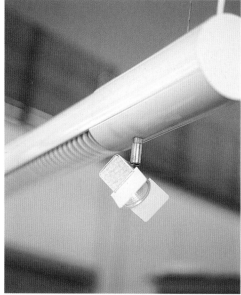

Above and above left **This contemporary tubular light not only illuminates the whole length of the breakfast bar and work surface but also has a spot that can be focused on a specific area.**

Far left **Steel's shiny surface acts like a mirror and reflects both natural and artificial light, but it is preferable to have a brushed or slightly matt finish rather than a true mirror-like effect because the latter may cause light to flare and glare, making it difficult to work with.**

Left **This kitchen in a cupboard is characterized by recessed spotlights with halogen bulbs, which create a clear white light above and a decorative, blue-tinted light below.**

Opposite, above **Recessed spotlights give task lighting above the hob and burners of the stove, while two decorative spots in the shelves on either side enhance the room's ambient lighting.**

Opposite, below **Fluorescent striplights come in a variety of sizes; this mini strip is a decorative feature as well as illuminating the worktop.**

up to 20 times longer than an incandescent bulb, do not cast such strong shadows as other lights and are cool so they will not add to the heat in a busy kitchen, but they are powerful and bright and should not be looked at directly.

A standard integrated lighting scheme involves the use of all three of these types of bulb to create various moods and settings. For example, for food preparation, fluorescent strips under units and halogen spots over the hob, sink and main island work area will be used in conjunction with halogen ceiling spots and ambient tungsten pendant lights. When food is cooking slowly in a casserole, for example, the main lights may be turned off and a specific task light left on so that the cook may come in and check on progress. When dinner is served, the ceiling spots may be turned off, and the wall and ceiling lights, both with tungsten bulbs,

can be dimmed to provide a soft background light that complements the candles on the table.

The kitchen is a greasy and steamy place so it is worth covering the base of recessed lights with clear glass shields or finding lights that have a cover already incorporated in the design. It will be easier to wipe the glass disc than to try to squeeze your hand into the recessed metal casing around the lamp for cleaning, and the disc may also offer a certain amount of protection for the light fitting.

Switches are best kept simple and easy to wipe. Fancy Victorian-style brass and wooden switches are difficult to operate if hands are sticky or soapy, whereas flat push switches can be activated with an elbow. If the kitchen is large, it may be wise to have switches for the main light on either side of the room so that you do not have to walk from one side to the other in the dark.

surfaces

After the lighting has been planned, the next decision you need to make is about the materials you want to use for the major surfaces in the room – the worktops and the cabinet doors. It is these large expanses of colour and texture that will dictate the character of the room more than any other element in the kitchen.

Opposite **A recess in a polished concrete worktop holds a chopping board securely in place.**
Below **Smooth curves give a softer and more modern finish.**
Right **Recessing hobs into the surface makes the area easier to clean.**
Below right **Concrete, painted MDF and maple add interest and variety.**

Worktops and splashbacks

The priorities for a worktop are that it should be hygienic and easy to wipe, as well as resilient enough to withstand hot pots and pans. It should be sufficiently wide to accommodate worktop machines and gadgets, and still leave space at the front for food preparation. The material used for the surface should also be sturdy so that the occasional sharp blade or skewer will not inflict lasting damage – although in theory all chopping should be done on a board, some-

times a knife may slip, so the surface should be resistant to sharp points.

Where possible a worktop should be made from one continuous length of material or, if that is not practical, with as few seams as are feasible. Crumbs and debris will accumulate in joins and seals, and they can be difficult to remove and clean out thoroughly. The length of worktop will be dictated by the layout and design of the kitchen, but guidelines indicate that an adequate work area should be at least 90 cm (36 in) long and preferably with easy access to the sink. If more than one person cooks in the kitchen at a time, each cook should ideally have a work surface of this size.

Splashbacks can be constructed from a continuous run of one material or made up from a collection of ceramic tiles with grouted joins. This area has, in recent times, become an additional hanging and storage place with spice racks and utensil rails being sited here. The splashback, as the name suggests, is the area where bits of flying cake mix or orange pulp will land when a mixing machine or fruit juicer are in action, so it should be a surface that is water resistant and easy to clean. The other area to take care with is the seam between the worktop and the splashback. There are flexible rubber sealants that can be piped along the join to create a filling, but a narrow varnished wooden strip, or a length of V-shaped plastic joining wedge may be as effective and possibly more attractive.

Materials that may be used for worktops and splashbacks include natural stone such as marble and granite, which generally come with a polished finish, and slate, which needs to be professionally sealed to prevent the stone from shaleing. For the splashback the stone need only be of veneer thickness as it does not have to withstand pressure or weight, but for the worktop it should be

Right **The clinical appearance of the steel worktop is softened by the dark wood of the unit fascias.** Opposite: top row from left **Marble's coolness makes it ideal for pastry-making. An integral draining board slopes down to the sink. Rounded edges are becoming more common in modern kitchens.** Middle row from left **Rails are ideal for hanging cloth, towel and oven gloves. Joins around sinks should be smooth and watertight. Thick work surfaces give a more definitive and expensive appearance.** Bottom row from left **Melamine and Pyrolave finishes come in many colours and can be customized to suit individual schemes. The area directly next to a sink should be carefully waterproofed. Steel can be used on most kitchen surfaces.**

thicker, so that it is more robust and solid. The coolness of stone is a boon in food preparation, especially for those who make their own pastry.

A recent innovation in stone surfaces is Pyrolave, made from volcanic lava stone. Pyrolave is made from a material that has been fired in the earth's own kiln, to temperatures that it is hard to comprehend, so it will easily withstand the hottest dishes and casseroles a domestic kitchen can come up with. Pyrolave is cut using high-pressure water jets. Surface design and texture can be applied via a computer, or it can be smoothed and polished to reveal its natural qualities.

Although stone is hardwearing and strong, and it will not be adversely affected by heat, the surface may be scratched by a sharp knife or blade. It is also easy to wipe clean, and unless it is sealed with a sensitive finish, it can be wiped down with disinfectant and powerful cleaning agents. The weight is a significant factor. A length of marble worktop, for example, can be extremely heavy, so make sure that the units or struts underneath them are sturdy enough to give ample support.

Wood is generally used for worktops or an inset into an area of worktop, but not often as a splashback. Recent reports suggest that wood has an inherent property that kills bacteria more readily than materials such as plastic, which makes it ideal for use in a food preparation area. Some wood is kiln dried and finished with oil or varnish to make it more resilient; other wood is left to dry naturally, and may be waxed or oiled. Although all work surfaces may be made of wood, some people choose to use it in conjunction with materials such as marble or steel so there are different surfaces for various parts of the food preparation routine.

Maintenance of wooden work surfaces is important; they should be wiped down frequently, (avoid harsh detergents) and be thoroughly dried after use. Although strong and long lasting, wood will be scored and marked by sharp knives and burned or scorched by hot pans. In some cases these blemishes can be removed by rubbing with sandpaper and re-applying the top finish.

Ceramic tiles are fine for splashback areas but really impractical for worktops. Ceramic tiles themselves are easy enough to wipe clean but the numerous grooves and ridges formed by the joins and grouting become full of dirt and the white grout soon becomes stained with tea, fruit juice or just grime. Unless you use a minimal number of very large ceramic tiles or are prepared to regularly bleach or re-grout between tiles, it is best to avoid

them on the worktop area. They may also chip or crack if a heavy pan or utensil is dropped on them.

Laminates are widely available, reasonably priced and come in a wide selection of colours, patterns and finishes, from plain white to marble. This surface is stain, abrasion and damp resistant, but sharp knives and hot pans can cause damage and scorch marks. It is sold in generous lengths, so there need only be minimal seams in the finished surface, which makes it good for both worktops and splashbacks. Laminate surfaces are low maintenance and long lasting, but avoid textured finishes – the small indentations and undulations, such as those used to achieve a wood grain effect, can be difficult to clean well.

Stainless steel is an increasingly popular worksurface and splashback material. Counter tops

tend to be custom made, although some manufacturers do have standard-size options. Sheets of steel can be formed to include integral sinks and pre-stamped drainage boards. These are advantageous because they cut down on the number of seams and joins. Where joins are unavoidable the two pieces of steel can be welded with an almost invisible seam. This is not only hygienic and practical; it also gives an attractive overall appearance.

In general terms, thicker steel is better for worktops; ideally it should be at least 0.9 mm thick. If it is any thinner than this the worktop may bend and flex under pressure.

Steel is hardwearing and, if well maintained, it will last a lifetime. Although hot pots will not affect the finish, scratches and dents may show, but lighter marks can be rubbed away with a gentle cream. Although scratches can be disheartening when the kitchen is new, in time the marks of general wear and tear blend together and are no

longer noticeable – in fact they can create a less hard, more polished effect. Some suppliers recommend non-grit cream cleaners to be used on steel surfaces as these reduce the incidents of scratching during regular cleaning.

Solid surfaces come in a variety of guises. Polyester, thermoplastic and acrylic resin finishes have made their way from the chemistry lab to the kitchen and offer a wide choice of durable, easy-to-clean surfaces. Also within this category are the surfaces made with natural materials and resins, re-constituted to form new products.

The new natural and man-made mix surfaces include Erbistone, which has a base of 95 per cent quartz, which results in a granite-like appearance with durability and hardness similar to the original stone. Corian®, which is constructed from two-thirds natural minerals combined with a high-performance acrylic, can be finished to appear as marble or granite or in a range of plain

Opposite **The bright blue wall complements the blue-white hue of the marble and adds warmth to an otherwise cool and clinical arrangement of white units with steel-fronted machines.**
Right and below far right **Vivid colours such as this pink come in melamine or other synthetic finishes, or may be created by professionally spray-painting MDF with car paint or specially mixed emulsion.**
Below right **The dramatic and unusual candy stripe was made by transferring a computer-generated photographic image onto melamine.**

colours. It also has the advantage of being very easy to bond to another piece, making seams and joins almost invisible.

Sheets of these materials can be grooved so that an integral draining board and sink can be created in the worktop, a smart way of banishing the difficult joins between the worktop and the sink rim. Some of these surfaces are slightly 'soft' and have warmer feel than the real stone surfaces. They can be scratched, but minor abrasions, if not too deep, can be easily sanded away. The main disadvantage of these materials is that they lack the lustre of real stone or marble, and it is recommended that they be installed by professionals, which may increase the overall price.

Unit doors

These will, in most kitchens, be the largest and most defining surface areas. The colour, style and type of door you choose will be a major part of the overall scheme. The doors will need to be hard-wearing – capable of withstanding kicks and bangs – as well as easy to clean. It is worth bearing in mind that the more ornate features, such as carved panels, beading and frames, that are added to the door, the more grooves and niches there will be in which grease and grime will collect, so this style of door will require more cleaning.

Wood is a popular finish for unit doors and it comes in three categories – hard woods, soft woods and veneers. Hard woods such as maple, oak and cherry are classic choices, but if the door is made of solid wood it can be heavy and expensive, though it should last for many years. This type of door is easy to clean with a damp cloth and mild detergent, but will, if sealed with oil or wax, need regular re-applications of the finish. Soft wood doors, such as those made from pine, are often stained or painted, as the wood is comparatively

cheap and in its natural state tends to be pale or yellow in colour, and lacking in interesting grain texture. If the doors are painted, stained or varnished, they are easy to clean with a damp cloth.

Veneers are thin layers of wood which are glued to a backing. They have the advantage of being lightweight (if they are applied to a lightweight backing material such as particleboard or MDF) and they are less expensive than solid wood but can create the same overall effect. With both veneers and solid wood it is important that the direction and line of the grain should match. Another point to remember is that all wood panels, doors and trimmings must be given time to acclimatize to the conditions of the kitchen or a room with similar humidity and temperatures so that it will not warp or crack when installed.

Laminates can be divided into two categories – high pressure and low pressure. High-pressure laminate is made from compressed resin and paper glued to a backing. Doors made from this material are generally plain, as it is not advisable to carve or rout the surface, but they are easy to clean and hardwearing. Low-pressure laminate, known as melamine, is cheaper, thinner and less durable than the high-pressure type, but is easy to clean and can be useful for rented apartments or in kitchens where a long-lasting surface is not required. Melamine is also often used to line the carcasses of kitchen units.

Polyester and resin-finished doors are usually in the top end of the price scale. A wide variety of pastel and brilliant colours can be achieved and given a high-gloss, almost lacquer-like, finish. These finishes are durable, but deep scratches and dents are difficult to repair.

If you are prone to boredom with your surroundings and are the type of person who likes to decorate regularly, it may be advisable to choose units dressed with a surface that can be painted or altered easily, rather than having to incur the expense of buying new doors each time you fancy a change. Simple faux plank or framed MDF or pine doors can be painted several times over with no detrimental effect. Laminates or other finishes with a high gloss may be difficult to paint or alter successfully. Painting MDF or cheaper wood doors will give the whole kitchen a fresh look – a good way of revitalizing a dated or well-worn room.

Opposite The contrast of the roughly hewn wood on the upper units and the smooth surface below gives an interesting emphasis to this kitchen.
Left The wood was left with its natural undulating curves rather than sawn into straight planks.
Below A small air grille allows air to circulate freely.
Bottom row from left. Unusual knobs accentuate the rough wood feel. The cupboards appear to be suspended from the beam but are also supported by metal struts. A freestanding cupboard echoes the finish of the wall unit.

Top row, from left **Opaque glass hides the contents of a cupboard but maintains a fresh appearance. The color and simplicity of these wooden knobs echo the work surface. Integral molded-steel drawer handles are tactile and stylish.**

Middle row, from left **Classic linear handles are ideal for long drawers. Small peg-style knobs are better on cupboard doors. Unusual ornate shapes should be reserved for units that are infrequently used.**

Left **Many metal handles are available in a choice of matt (shown here) or highly polished finishes.**

Right **Sliding panel doors can hide whole areas of a kitchen and can be used to cover sections of floor-to-ceiling shelving. These recessed-disc handles slot neatly into the face of the panel.**

Opposite **Fine metal mesh gives the impression of a door but allows light and air to circulate; it is also used in front of the fridge for a uniform effect. If buying sheets of mesh from a DIY store, ensure that it has a lacquered finish to prevent rusting.**

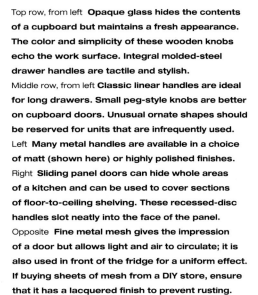

plumbing

In these days when dishwashers are increasingly popular a good size, single sink may fulfil all your water supply and drainage needs, but in a busy household two sinks may be needed to cope with overflow dishes and food preparation. It may also suit your work style to have two sinks, but in different areas. For example, in a large kitchen it could be useful to have a food preparation sink near the fridge and vegetable rack and another near the dishwasher and china cupboards for hand-washing and storing fine glass and china or cutlery.

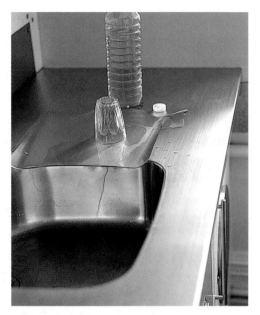

Sinks

There are various shapes of sink to consider, from the single, which, if it is a generous-sized bowl may be enough if used in conjunction with a dish-washer, to the multi sink. The double sink is still very popular, with one bowl used for washing and the other for rinsing. The triple sink usually incorpo-rates a waste disposal unit in the centre. Slide-over chopping boards and draining racks can make practical use of the space when not in use.

Round sinks are not so popular in kitchens because they do not make the best use of the space available, although they can be a good sec-ond sink for vegetable preparation. Another rarity, but one that can be useful in an awkward corner area, is the angular sink. The angular unit usually comprises two sinks set in a diamond shape with the draining board in the triangular space at the top between the two sink points.

Integral sinks are made of the same material as the worktop, Corian® for example, but for stand-alone sinks steel is still universally popular. As with a steel worktop, it is best to buy the thickest steel you can for a sink, preferably around 0.8 to 0.9 mm thick. This will have less give and be less noisy than a thinner sink. Finish is important too. Steel sinks come in a satin finish, which is matt, and a high polish, which is more likely to show up battle scars and scratches.

Opposite Plumbing taps and an adjustable water spout above the sink allows unhindered access.
Above left **A good draining surface that leads directly into the sink is an important feature.**
Above right **Lever taps are easy to operate with greasy or soapy hands.**
Right **The sink or sinks should be situated within the heart of the working area.**

Ceramic sinks are also manufactured and popular in such settings as Traditional and Simple Country kitchens. Original large oblong Belfast sinks can be found in antique shops and sales rooms, although modern copies are easier to track down. Porcelain-enamelled sinks with a cast-iron base come in various sizes and colours with a glossy enamel finish. These sinks are attractive and hardwearing but may stain and chip if a hard item is dropped onto the surface. Granite, marble and stone sinks can also be found but are rare and usually made to order.

Non-integral sinks are usually mounted into the work surface and there are a number of ways to approach this. Self-rimming sinks are finished with a rolled edge which can be set directly into the opening in the worktop and sealed with a waterproof edge. Under-mounted sinks are usually installed into stone or solid worktops, so that the hard worktop has a smooth, polished or finished edge and the sink is placed directly beneath.

Taps and spouts

There is a wide variety of taps and spouts on offer and the best way to decide what you want is to analyse how you use them, what feels most comfortable in your hands and finally which style seems appropriate to the look of your kitchen. There are very sophisticated combinations available, from those that are hands-free, turned on and off by breaking an infrared beam, to others that

Opposite, clockwise from top left **This shallow, sloping sink is an integral part of the worktop. A freestanding tap in a utility area of the kitchen is useful for filling buckets and large vases. A stainless steel sink is recessed neatly below a wooden worktop. Double sinks are useful for busy kitchens. Cleaning agents are best stored under the sink, well away from food stuffs. The shape of the sink is a personal choice but round bowls are unusual and attractive. Mixer taps are an increasingly popular choice. An extendable hose that pulls out of the main tap can be used to direct a powerful jet of water. A hose is also useful for washing the surfaces around the sink.**
Above **Lever taps can be turned on accidentally so it is important to turn them off properly.**
Far left **Sinks are often placed in front of a window so that daylight can provide illumination.**
Left **A large and small sink may suit your needs better than two large ones.**

Above **A tap with a single adjustable spout is ideal for supplying water to a double sink. The spout can be moved out of the way to allow large vessels and buckets to be filled at the sink.**

Above right **Mixer taps make it possible for water of exactly the right temperature to be obtained directly from the spout.**

Right **The shape of the spout is a personal choice; this arching curve has a pleasing line.**

Opposite, above left **Choose the colour and style of tap and spout to complement the scheme in the rest of your kitchen.**

Opposite, above right **A spout of this type can be swung away from the centre of the sink – an advantage when washing fragile china dishes or glass which might accidentally knock against the base of a rigid, centrally positioned spout.**

Opposite, below **Pipes are deliberately exposed as a style feature. This arrangement also gives easy access in case of a leak or blockage.**

offer a pull-out spout with brush and variable water pressure options. This fitting looks attractive and exciting but it may be an unnecessary luxury if you use the dishwasher every day and buy pre-prepared vegetables.

To assess grip and general tactile qualities, it is best to have a hands-on trial of the tap. For those who suffer from hand-mobility problems or who do a lot of baking, lever taps are a good option. They are easy to turn on with a forearm or elbow, whereas a grip-and-turn tap will become covered with ingredients, making it difficult to manipulate and to clean later. But check that your local buildings regulations allow for domestic installation of these industrial-design taps – they can be wasteful of water.

The classic lines of a standard spout will suit most styles of kitchen. If possible get an adjustable spout so that you can direct the water into the corners of the sink for easy cleaning. A gooseneck spout has a more acute angle of curve and is longer and more slender than the standard design. It is not a good idea for a busy sink as the flow produces a narrow jet of water, but it can be attractive in a low-use sink in a Traditional-style kitchen.

Taps and spouts come in a number of finishes, including chrome, brass, coloured epoxy coating, pewter and nickel. Chrome is most popular, and it is available in matt, brushed and high-polish finish. It is easily buffed up and made to sparkle with a dry soft cloth and is hard wearing and durable. Brass can be attractive but make sure it is lacquered or finished with an epoxy seal otherwise you will have to spend time cleaning and polishing the taps and spout. The finishes seal in the shine and take away the effort of mainte-nance. Enamel coatings are applied over the metal base and fired at a high temperature to fix them. These finishes come in many colours, but the simplest white finish is the most popular and least obtrusive.

Filters and disposal systems

If you are installing a new sink you may like to add an integral water filter that will purify the cold water as it passes through the system. If you use a lot of water for drinking or in cooking then having a filter fitted to the tap can save a lot of time and bother filling up filter jugs. There are various types of filters on the market but basically the standard fixture has a filter, which extracts and decontaminates, fitted beneath the sink.

Many people find a waste disposal unit a useful feature in a sink system, so that vegetable and smaller items of biodegradable matter can be readily and easily disposed of, saving time and the effort of taking out wastebins. Also the instant disposal of waste that may decay saves rotting and unpleasant smells, especially during hot summer periods. Some people, however, particularly keen gardeners, prefer to recycle their kitchen waste into compost, in which case a separate bin can be installed under the sink in which organic waste matter is disposed of.

Dishwashers

Modern machines have re-configured interiors with racks and shelving systems that allow space for larger and bulkier loads, and built-in convection driers that circulate hot air, causing moisture to evaporate – quicker and more effective than older methods.

Machines with two spray arms, one at the top and the other at the bottom are most often recommended as this ensures good overall distribution of water. At the bottom of most

Below **Taps with extendable hoses can be fitted with a showerhead for rinsing fruit and vegetables.**
Right **This style of dishwasher recalls a filing cabinet with pull-out drawers.**
Below right **Even in a kitchen with a dishwasher, draining space beside the sink is indispensable.**
Opposite **A mix of unfitted pieces, including a retro wooden sink, define the character of this rustic kitchen.**

machines is a filter which catches larger particles of food. This should be regularly cleaned.

Many dishwashers can now be concealed behind panels. Units with the control panel on the inner rim of the door are most suitable. These concealed controls mean that the outer door can be flush with the other unit doors.

Stainless steel interiors cope well with the heat and stress of high-power washes but some metals, such as silver, will tarnish in reaction to the steel, so it is best to handwash silver or silver-plate cutlery.

Check how quiet the machine is in operation; there is nothing worse than being kept awake after a dinner party or trying to hold a telephone conversation in competition with the spraying and whirring of the dishwasher. Most modern machines are reasonably quiet as manufacturers now use more effective insulation.

appliances

Opposite **Refrigerators are growing in size and importance. Many come in a selection of colours and shapes designed to make them an integral part of the overall scheme.**
Top left **Classic enamel-fronted stoves or ranges may be run on a variety of different fuels.**
Top right **Hobs with smooth glass covers are simple to wipe clean when cold.**
Above left **Washing machines and other bulky equipment can be concealed behind unit doors.**
Above right **Stacking ovens and microwaves in a wall-mounted unit saves space but there must be adequate ventilation to prevent overheating.**

Modern appliances are designed not only to be efficient and attractive; increasingly manufacturers are responding to cultural demands and taking environmental issues on board. They are producing more machines that are energy saving or efficient and low in if not free of products such as chloro-fluoro-carbons (CFCs). Before choosing your appliances – especially cookers, hobs and stoves – check what sort of power is available. While there will be no problem with electrical supply it is possible you may not have a gas supply outlet in your kitchen. If this is the case you will have to call in a registered gas fitter to install one, and this will add to your overall cost of the cooker.

Cookers and hobs

There are a number of combinations for cooker power. For example there is dual power, which offers a gas hob and a self-cleaning electric oven. Another popular feature in an electric oven is the convection fan: this circulates the heat evenly so that each shelf or rack maintains the same level of heat. This is useful if you are baking several racks of cakes – there is no need to open the oven door and move the racks up and down. Also, if you are cooking several dishes with different flavours, such as a fish pie and a fruit flan, the flavours should not mingle or taint the other dishes.

Gas ovens also offer a wide variety of modern features, such as an infrared grill which can achieve temperatures of up to 1500 degrees, which will quickly sear food, replacing the standard grill and charcoal-effect barbecue style grills.

Appliances evolve and are upgraded on a regular basis, and this can be seen in hobs. Electric and gas burners used to be the norm but recently new types of heat sources have changed the appearance and efficiency of the hob. Gas is still popular, both in the traditional removable rack burner and the sealed burner. The sealed unit is marginally more expensive but is easier to clean. Choose a hob with an electric pilot light ignition – it can save the grind of trying to re-light the pilot when it goes out, and is safer than using matches.

Ceramic and glass hob tops are easy to clean and are among the sleekest-looking. The smooth top prevents bits of food from falling down between rings and niches and, although fragile-looking, the glass is tough and resilient. This type of hob can be heated by radiant, halogen or magnetic induction coils. Magnetic induction is most like gas in that it can quickly be adjusted from high to low with almost instant effect.

Electric coil hobs have been around for some time, but they are still popular. The electric element can be simply the coiled rings which glow when hot or they can be concealed or integrated into a metal plate which diffuses the heat. Gas hobs have often been favoured over electric ones because they offer greater control.

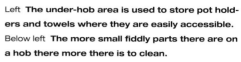

Left **The under-hob area is used to store pot hold-ers and towels where they are easily accessible.**
Below left **The more small fiddly parts there are on a hob there more there is to clean.**
Below **Larger fridges have integral ice making and cool drink facilities.**
Opposite **This hob area combines a hot plate, gas burners and a griddle.**

When choosing the configuration of your hob opt for a variety of ring strengths. Thermal heat is measured in British Thermal Units, known as Btus. The higher the number, the more intense the heat, so a 600 Btu rating will simmer milk, whereas 12,000 Btus will boil water and heat woks.

New hob accessories have been developed to make the professional range more suitable for domestic cooking. For example, the old raised hob grille that was difficult to balance a large pot on can be replaced with a closed grilled plate and special cradle grilles to accommodate woks.

There are hundreds of types of cookers, from the industrial style freestanding cooker and the domestic adaptation of it, to the Victorian range. Traditional-style ranges mostly now run on oil, natural or propane gas, or they can be adapted to run off low-rate off-peak electricity. They operate on a heat storage principal; the ovens and hot plates have thermostatically controlled temperatures. The cast-iron lining to the lids and ovens are self-cleaning, as spillages and deposits of food burn off, leaving only ash behind. These cookers are heavy and require a level ground and an outside flue for ventilation. They can also be linked to the domestic heating system, but in the summer when you may need to turn the stove off you could need an alternative source of warmth and cooking.

Microwaves

Countertop microwaves can be a great asset to busy working people and families with a small baby or a number of young school children who need meals served promptly and at differing times. As food is generally taken from the fridge or freezer and then placed in the microwave it makes sense to position it near these appliances. Do not place the mircowave next to other machines that generate heat, such as a wall-mounted oven, as the heat may affect the microwave's performance. Also, if

the microwave is to be wall mounted in a cupboard or fitted into a unit make sure there is adequate ventilation. When buying a microwave look for features such as an extra shelf for simultaneous heating. And do not forget to check your crockery before using it. Is it microwave safe?

Extractor hoods and fans

Do not skimp on a ventilation unit; not only will it remove smells and steam but in the process it will keep the temperature of the kitchen bearable and the atmosphere pleasant to work and eat in.

The size and strength of the ventilation system will depend on the floor area and capacity of the kitchen and the amount and type of cooking you do. If you only boil the kettle twice a day and cook using a microwave then a powerful fan is unnecessary. The strength of an extractor fan is gauged in metric litres per second, or cubic feet per minute, abbreviated as CFM. Check with the supplier that the ventilator is strong enough for your needs.

Above **Make sure that you have adequate space and ventilation around a microwave oven.**
Right and opposite **The capacity of the extractor or ventilator should be matched to the size of the hob below it and the volume of heat produced. For maximum efficiency, fit the device to the height recommended by the manufacturer. Some extractors have filters that use charcoal or similar purifying agents; these will have to be changed from time to time, so they must be accessible.**

Opposite **In a kitchen combined with a living or dining area, an effective extractor is essential not only to remove cooking smells but also to reduce smoke and condensation.**
Left **Extractor casings can either complement the cooker and be in the same finish, or be disguised so that they blend in with the wall colour or finish.**
Below left **Wall-mounted items such as extractor hoods should be free of sharp edges; otherwise, especially if set at head height, they could be a source of painful bumps.**

There are two main types of extractor. One is the updraft hood that is positioned over the hob and sucks the steam and odours away from the pots and pans as it rises. Updraft extractors should be ducted through an outside wall or up a disused chimney so the moisture and smells are properly dispersed. This type of hood should be carefully positioned; if it is too close to the hob the steam may waft out on either side of the hood, if it is too far away the steam will disperse before reaching it. To check that the vent is well positioned – ideally about 75cm (30 inches) above the hob – simply boil a pan of water on the hob and watch the vapour rise to the vent or place a sheet of paper on the unlit hob and see if it rises when the vent is turned on. Updraft systems are normally cased in a hood. The hood can be tailored to match the other units, or be made into a feature by giving it a casing in contrast to the rest of the room, such as copper or brushed steel. In contemporary kitchens the hood can be a sculpted feature and a focal point of the room, following the idea that if it is a large feature make the most of it rather than trying to hide it.

The other type of ventilation system is the downdraft, which is generally built into the back of the hob top or island unit with a grille arrangement at the back. This type of system is less obtrusive than a hood, but is not as effective since it filters and recirculates the air rather than expelling it.

Extractor fans such as the updraft and downdraft, as well as those plumbed directly into the wall or window, can be noisy, so check with the supplier how intrusive the noise level will be. There are super-quiet extractors on the market; these have extra insulation which tends to make them more costly.

Fridges and freezers

Consider the size of fridge you need. Do you require a large capacity machine with ice-making and cold water facilities or would a side-by-side combination of two smaller units suit your needs and the size and dimensions of your room better? Do not buy a huge upright fridge-freezer that will take up most of a tiny kitchen when a smaller version or a combination of machines may give you more valuable worktop space.

Modern fridges and freezers are increasingly energy efficient, using less than half the power they did a decade ago. Many are now CFC-free designs which eliminate the harmful ingredients that damage the earth's ozone layer. Many fridges have zonal refrigeration, which means that within one unit there

are areas of different degrees of coolness – chill at the base, cool in the centre and cold on top. A labour-saving frost-free facility cuts out the task of de-frosting the freezer manually as the machine is capable of regulating the humidity and temperature so that there is no icy build-up.

Fridges and freezers that are destined to slot in between units in a fitted kitchen are generally shallower, around 60 cm (24 in) deep, than the equivalent freestanding appliances, which are between 70 to 85 cm (28 to 34 in) deep, because the built-in variety are reduced to make them flush with the units that surround it, whereas the free-standing fridge-freezer can stand proud of cabinets or tables that may surround it.

There is also an increased demand for custom-made panels to add to the front of built-in appliances so that the fascia of the fridge blends in with the rest of the units. Freestanding machines are generally chosen with a standard white, steel or coloured panel which will tone in with the main colours of the room rather than matching the style or finish of the array of units.

As well as the straightforward chilling, freezing and cooling features of the conventional appliance, there are a number of recent innovations such as the wine cooler and under-counter fridge drawers. The wine cooler can be a tall cellar-style unit or a smaller 60-bottle machine that fits under a work-top and is a standard 60 cm (24 in) unit size. As

well as wine bottles, bottles of mineral water and soft drinks may also be stored. Most of these appliances have a temperature dial and variable temperature zones so that the degree of coolness can be varied to suit the type of wine being stored or your personal taste.

Fridge drawers are ideal for keeping fresh fruit and vegetables lightly chilled; they are perfect for island or peninsular units. A single may provide enough space – if not two drawers can be installed one on top of the other to provide double the capacity and a variety of chill and cool settings.

Top row, from left **If you enjoy entertaining, consider having a refrigerator devoted solely to chilling beers, mineral water, vodka, wine and glasses. By recessing the fridge-freezer into the wall, valuable space has been saved in a galley kitchen. Its simple steel exterior makes this large unit seem less bulky and dominant than it otherwise might.**
Above left **Refrigerators should be regularly defrosted and thoroughly cleaned to prevent crumbs and particles of food from going mouldy.**
Above **Adjustable fridge shelves are convenient for storing bulky items.**
Opposite **Retro-style fridges in various colours are now being made by some leading manufacturers.**

accessories

Opposite **A Dualit toaster is a timeless classic. Many modern metal gadgets are treated with a protective film which means they can be wiped rather than polished.**

Left **Some juicers are for citrus fruits only, while others will take vegetables, separating the juice from the fibre and pips.**

Below left **Espresso and cappuccino machines can be very modern and high-tech or, like this one, have an old-fashioned appearance.**

Bottom left **Glass blender jugs can be washed in boiling water and will not cloud or scratch in the way plastic or synthetic jugs often do.**

Below **This manual citrus juicer is an attractive piece of equipment that can be left on display.**

Bottom **This sturdy and durable mixer is the up-to-date version of an old-fashioned machine.**

In addition to large-scale appliances there is a vast array of smaller scale machines, tools, utensils and gadgets available that make a cook's working life easier and more fun. Machines should be carefully chosen, primarily for their use and function, but also for their good looks. Apparatus that is going to be left out on the counter top should be attractive and contribute to the overall appearance of the room. Less attractive but nonetheless vital and useful pieces of machinery should be stowed away in drawers and cupboards.

Any items that are used frequently should be stored on the surface or kept adjacent to the worktop. Other machines that are heavy to move can be left on the surface under a cover to camouflage their bulk and protect the machine from steam and grease. If it is a machine that is rarely used, could it be stored elsewhere and brought into the kitchen when needed, so freeing storage space where it may be more vitally needed?

Worktop machines

When choosing these smaller appliances, try running through an imaginary day. For example, on rising the first task is breakfast. Do you drink juice from a carton or do you prepare it fresh? If so would an easy hand-lever non-electrical squeezer do or would a small electric juicer be better? Consider how much time you have to wash and dry the gadget after use, and decide whether the machine and its accessories should be dishwasher proof.

What is your regular hot drink – cappuccino, espresso or instant coffee, tea or hot water with lemon? For cappuccino and espresso a specific machine is the quickest and most effective option. A toaster offers the speediest way of toasting muffins, crumpets or bread, but if you have more time the grill on the cooker will do the same job.

After breakfast, consider other meals and their preparation as an aid to selecting further equipment. A blender is useful for making lunchtime soups and may be combined with a detachable gadget for grinding coffee beans or nuts. These facilities may be offered as part of a food processor package, but if you make soup on a regular basis the blender may be easier to use and to wash up. A food processor can be bulky and fiddly to clean, and it may be better replaced with a selection of smaller individual machines.

Top row, from left **This modern round-bodied kettle sits snugly and safely on the trivet over a gas burner. A basic old-fashioned cast-iron kettle has a traditional charm. Stainless steel pans can be expensive, but they will last a lifetime and they will not taint or affect food as aluminium pans can.**
Above, from left **Choose the right size equipment to suit your needs – this simple filter makes coffee for one a quick and easy business. Heat-resistant glass is now used for many items of cookware; this glass teapot brings a new look to a classic vessel. There are few things more welcoming than the smell of fresh coffee brewing, and this stove-top percolator will ensure a ready supply.**
Opposite **In this modern streamlined kitchen all the utensils on display are all suitably good looking. But if you hang utensils on the backplate you must take care when reaching for them across the hob when the burners are in use.**

If you are an avid fan of oriental cuisine an electric rice steamer is a boon, and for grinding herbs and spices for these dishes a pestle and mortar is essential. Salad lovers may find a vegetable spinner useful for getting excess water out of lettuce and other leaves. Pasta fans might favour a pasta maker and cutter. Bread makers that prove the dough are also labour saving but tend to be bulky, while yoghurt makers are once again popular with the renewed interest in healthy eating.

Basic equipment

Standard kitchen equipment should include a good range of pots and pans to cater for various types and amounts of cooking. Aluminium pans may cause certain foods to discolour or taint the flavour.

Stainless steel is light and durable and copper, though expensive, is a good conductor of heat and attractive to display. Copper pans are good for sauces and flambéd dishes. Cast-iron casseroles and pans are heavy but good for slow cooking and are perfect for cooking on a range.

Frying pans are another basic piece of equipment. Non-stick linings make them easier to use and to wash up. Ideally a frying pan should not be too heavy as you should be able to lift it easily and move it on and off the heat as you need to. Wok cooking has become increasingly popular: it requires little fat and cooks noodles, vegetables and other ingredients quickly. Some woks come with domed lids that keep juices and steam within the pan, making the food moist and succulent.

There are many other specialist pots and pans such as asparagus boilers and fish kettles but these are ancillaries and not essential to the basic kitchen battery.

But good quality sharp knives are an essential. Carbon steel blades have to be carefully dried and cared for as they can be prone to rust spots, but they last indefinitely and can be easily sharpened. Ordinary stainless steel blades will not rust, but they may be more difficult to sharpen. All knives should be stored with care, preferably in a block or a rack, both to avoid cut fingers and to keep blades sharp. Magnetic holders that can be screwed to a wall near a work surface are also good. Using a sharpening steel – a long, textured rod on a handle – is the easiest and quickest way to revitalize the edge of a blade, but if you are not used to using a steel ask someone in a reputable kitchen equipment store to show you how it is done, because there is a knack to it.

Sieves, colanders and draining spoons are also useful for separating food from fluids, whether they be water, stock or sauce. Wooden spoons and spatulas are best used for stirring and are preferable for use in enamel or non-stick surfaced pots as the wood will not scratch or damage the finish. A fish slice is designed for turning and lifting fish and meat as well as any longer roll or sponge puddings, as it gives good leverage and a flat support. Ladles and large spoons with long handles will enable you

Above **For crushing dried herbs and spices an old-fashioned pestle and mortar cannot be faulted.**
Far left **A good sharp knife is essential and a range of different sizes and types of knives gives you the choice of getting the right tool for the job, but sharp blades should be carefully stored. This magnetic knife rack holds the blades in place, leaving the handles free.**
Left **Weighing scales come in many guises – this one has a traditional appearance.**

Left **Old butcher's blocks like this can be found through specialist suppliers. Clean them in boiling water before use and avoid detergents unless specifically designed for wood use.**

Below **Copper pans are popular with keen cooks because the metal is a good heat conductor, so the pan warms quickly. This type of pan is often used for making sauces and custards.**

Bottom row, from left **A lip on a chopping board stops it from sliding across the surface when in use. Identical glass jars present a pleasing uniformity on a shelf, but the ingredients they contain and reveal should be attractive, too. Keep all regularly used utensils in a ceramic or stoneware jar which can be regularly washed.**

to stir hot dishes at a distance from the heat source and to take larger quantities of stock or sauce out of a container. A large fork, again with a long handle, will make prodding and turning roasts easier. Graters from small for nutmeg to large for cheese and breadcrumbs will also give a more professional finish to food preparation.

Weighing scales are useful not just for gauging cake ingredients but also for weighing dried beans and pulses and pasta to ensure that you get the right quantity. Some recipes require spoon measurements; you should not use any old spoon in your drawer but have a set of specifically calibrated spoons. A set of measuring cups is also a useful tool.

Waste disposal

Waste disposal is a major part of life in the kitchen – with more and more packaging and pre-prepared foods the bin seems to fill ever more rapidly. Also, with a strong cultural move toward recycling and organic gardening, waste is more frequently divided into different lots so that each type can be sent to the right end. For example, a small bin for fruit and vegetable peelings, egg shells and other bio-degradable matter can be taken directly to a compost heap. Aluminium cans, flattened by stamping on them or with a mechanical press, can be recycled. Glass can also be separated out – some recycling depots require it to be divided into brown, green and white – for re-use, as can newspapers, magazines and printed paper waste.

Top right **Storing pots with their lids makes it simpler to pair them up.**
Right **Old-fashioned butcher's hooks are efficient, movable hangers.**
Far right **Having whisks and ladles near the hob saves time and effort.**
Below **Keep pans within easy reach.**
Below right **Herbs and spices stored in an orderly way are easy to locate.**
Opposite, clockwise from left **A good-sized bin is essential for bulky waste. Individual recycling bins hold wet and dry waste separately. Pedal-operated fliptop bins are useful when your hands are full.**

cabinets

The kitchen is a fully functioning work station, and the day-to-day activity of cooking and producing meals generates a huge amount of equipment, from tools and utensils to plates and cups, and of course the raw material – food. All of this must be stored in a systematic and organized way so that you can locate what you need quickly and access it easily. The primary function of the main furniture in the kitchen – the cabinets – is storage. But there are other considerations when choosing cabinets than merely containing all your clutter: storage cannot dominate the room to such an extent that there is insufficient space left for the food preparation itself, and because they are such an important feature in the room the units must look good and work well with the appliances you have chosen.

Not all cabinets need to be new or fitted. An unfitted kitchen is an ideal place to use a mix of old and new pieces of furniture. An old chest of drawers can be used for linen and lightweight storage and an armoire or cabinet for larger items. With this style of layout, cabinets of all shapes and sizes can be brought together to form a useful storage and work area. Small units can be jacked up on pedestals or bases so that they form a level surface with other furniture, and if required a length of worktop can be laid over a number of such units to create a continuous solid work area and to prevent bits of food and crumbs falling down between the individual cupboards.

Cabinet layout

Units can be installed in a number of ways. The simplest is a straight rows of cupboards top and bottom, but to add interest and variety the wall units could be staggered so that some are higher than others. For example, over an area of worktop where small appliances and machines are used the

Opposite **Shelves can be subdivided with small internal racks to give extra capacity.**
Clockwise, from top left **This mobile butcher's block combines a work surface with useful storage. A pull-down container in front of the sink holds pot scrubbers and cloths. Ingredients and dried foods can be attractive if well displayed. Solid doors on the lower units hide utilitarian equipment, while glass panels on the doors above give a less dense appearance. Where possible, store items close to where they will be used. Glass-fronted units allow decorative items to be put on show.**

units could be lower (but still giving easy access to the work surfaces), making it easy to get machines in and out of the units. Where the units are to be used for storing items that are seldom used, they could be placed higher up the wall. But this staggered effect needs to be carefully planned so that it looks balanced and purposeful rather than random and accidental.

Among a wall of solid doored units it can be light relief to have a series of open shelves. The shelves can be used to display cookery books, attractive gadgets or china, but open shelves are best sited away from the hob where steam and grease may cause damage to books and grime to accumulate on china. Under-unit shelves can be useful places for attractive stainless steel or enamel cookware to be shown off. The tools will be readily accessible and they will add colour and interest among a run of units.

As well as shelves, plate and wine racks can be used to interrupt the line of units. In a small kitchen a plate rack for drying and storing dishes could be placed above a sink and between two upper, wall-mounted units. Otherwise it could be positioned over the worktop and be an attractive as well as practical storage feature. Wine racks are often built into residual or leftover space where fitted units cannot be accommodated. These wine racks are generally for show rather than serious use. They may house a dozen or so bottles of wine

used for cooking rather than serious drinking; the temperature of the kitchen will vary enormously, a less than ideal situation for maintaining quality wine in good condition.

Interior details

Within the units there can be a number of useful interior fittings to divide the space available, such as drawer dividers and cutlery trays (these can be standard or two tier with a sliding top layer and a rigid base that gives double capacity). Extra deep pan drawers for storing large pans and their lids are often lined with ridged rubber mats which stop the pots and lids sliding about and marking the drawer – these can be easily removed and cleaned when they get grubby. When choosing these interior facilities check that they will be adjacent to the areas where they will be most in use.

Opposite page, top **A mix of drawer and cupboard storage is used as a base for this hob.**

Opposite page, bottom row from left **A chequerboard of units created by alternating glass-and-steel doors with solid ones creates an interesting visual effect. Open shelves are prone to gather dust, so items on display should be regularly wiped down. Sliding drawers are useful for heavy items.**

Above, left and right **Tall condiment cupboards are designed to hold small bottles of essences, spice packets and bottles of flavoured oils; the shelves are short but ideal for small packages. An end cabinet with a fold-up panel is a good place to store machines that are in frequent use.**

Left **A simple steel rack set into a recess in the wall, with deep open-mesh shelves and an opaque glass door, makes a cheap form of storage.**

If fruit and vegetables or other perishable goods are to be stored on racks or shelves you will be able to keep them for much longer if they have plenty of air circulating around them. If you rest them on hard solid surfaces in closed drawers moisture from the fruit or vegetables will cause mould to form more readily. Wire mesh drawers are a good option, as are natural wicker baskets. In both cases the open weave prevents any moisture accumulating. The main disadvantage is that small pieces of broken peel or soil may work their way through the open

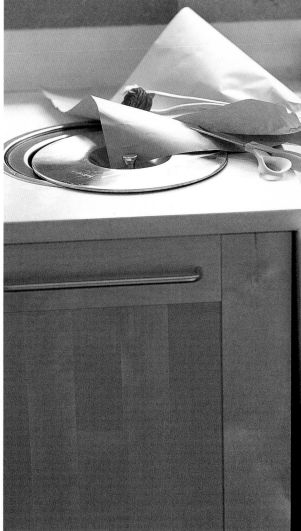

Opposite, top left **A trolley is a useful accessory, especially in a big kitchen, where it can be used to transport ingredients from one side of the room to another. If the trolley is the right height, the top can also be used as additional work space.**
Opposite, top right **Items often used consecutively, such as a mixing bowl, baking tins and a cooling rack, are best stored together so they can be taken out and replaced at the same time.**
Opposite, bottom row from left **Glass shelves appear almost invisible and make a good support for a display of fragile and decorative ware such as glass. These glasses are stored in a drawer lined with a non-slip mat. Subdivided shallow drawers are ideal for segregating different types of cutlery.**
Left **In cabinets or drawers where jams or other sticky jars or bottles are kept, a removable, washable base mat is helpful.**
Above **This cabinet façade hides a waste bin, the lid of which is set into the worktop.**

spaces and tumble to the bottom of the cupboard or onto another shelf. A fine mesh panel inserted between the drawers would collect this debris while still allowing a free flow of air. Wicker can also be hard to clean; wire mesh can simply be wiped over with a damp cloth but wicker will need a scrub with a hard-bristled brush.

Think about the construction of drawers and the type of runners you will need. For drawers that will hold lightweight items such as tea towels, table linen or cutlery, plastic runners are suitably smooth running and they are relatively inexpensive, but for drawers destined to hold cast-iron pots the runners should be sturdier. Metal is more costly than plastic but it will withstand the pressures of a heavier load. Metal runners should run smoothly but they may require a little lubrication if they become old and stubborn.

Top left **These wire mesh trays prevent vegetables from becoming sweaty or mouldy as they allow air to circulate freely around the produce.**

Top right **It is a good idea to put a heat-proof layer of protection between an oven and a cabinet in which you are planning to store foodstuffs that might be affected by high temperatures.**

Above and right **Baskets make a change from solid drawers, and they can be lifted out to carry linens directly to the table. They would also be good for fruit and vegetables as, like mesh ones, they allow the contents to 'breathe'.**

Opposite **A good mix of wall and floor cabinets, open shelving, drawers and mobile storage makes a hardworking and attractive kitchen.**

Too many drawers can be inefficient – you are limited by their size and shape as to what they will hold and they may tempt you to fill them with unnecessary clutter – so analyse exactly where you will need them and what you will keep in them. You may find that a single five-drawer unit and one or two units with single drawers above open cupboard space is enough. Many items such as cutlery and linen for formal dinners could be stored elsewhere, leaving space in the kitchen for essentials.

Beneath the unit doors is the area where the kickboard is situated. In most kitchens this board finishes the units and links them to the floor, hiding the legs or supports underneath the cabinet and preventing dirt finding its way into spaces that are awkward to clean. But in a small kitchen where space is really precious, this area can be used to house a number of small drawers that can accommodate frying pans and other less bulky pieces of kitchen equipment.

Cupboard doors

The contents of a cabinet need not necessarily be standard storage. Cupboard doors can be used to conceal what goes on behind them and to put a good face on something that is not attractive. For example, to maintain the flow of units and to give an overall symmetry to a kitchen, a fake door panel can disguise a wastebin or a washing machine, and similarly a mock drawer front could hide a pull-out,

Above **An unusual wedge-shaped hanging rack projects items on the upper rungs, making it easier to select and remove objects. The depth and size of items can be graduated from the top down so that the area directly in front of the stove is not obscured or hindered by large pots or pans, and items most often used are close to hand.**
Above right **Drawers don't have to be square: these rounded metal mesh drawers create an softer edge to the overall unit façade and bring a different texture and finish into the scheme.**
Right **Bits of debris may fall through so a layer of mesh screen is used to make a sliding lid.**

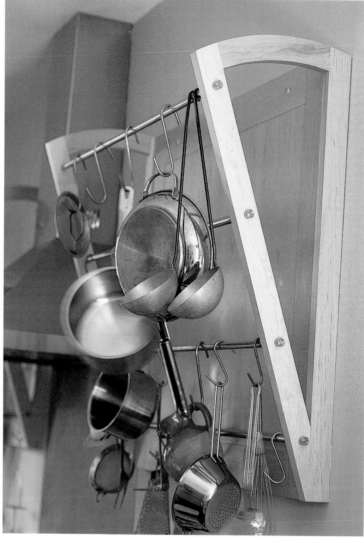

extending table or chopping board. A solid door, whether it is made of wood, laminate or MDF, is the most useful option for creating a range of versatile storage like this, as you are not limited as to what you can store behind it.

However, having a kitchen furnished completely with solid doors can look heavy and clumsy. Having just one or two cupboards with glazed doors will not pose too many restrictions on your storage arrangements, because there will always be some objects in the kitchen that are attractive enough to be put on show. Decorative clear or opaque and sandblasted glass panels can be an interesting addition to a kitchen, adding light to a dark or small room. With improvements in safety, and the development of reinforced and laminated types, glass is now suitable for general use.

Above left **Keep fragile items stored together and heavier, more robust objects in another place; mixing china and cast-iron pots in the same drawer will lead to breakages.**

Above **Metal equipment can benefit from being stored over a warm area such as a cooker because the rising heat will help to dry out any moisture left after washing, but unless they are used frequently they will gather grease and dust.**

Left **Narrow spaces can be utilized with pull-out racks like this one. They can be used for keeping condiments and spices or cleaning materials.**

furniture

The furniture in a kitchen caters for the subsidiary functions of the room: dining and, to a lesser extent, relaxing. Stools, tables and chairs in a kitchen may be informal, but they should be chosen to complement the overall style of decoration. The furniture may revolve around a selection of colours in the same design, or comprise a mix of styles with a similar theme, using the same materials – wood or chrome, say. Old and new pieces can often be mixed successfully. For example, in a kitchen where there is a breakfast bar area high stools will be the most appropriate seating, but around a table in the same room where more formal dining may take place the seating will more likely be provided by chairs. It may not be necessary to have matching stools and chairs; in fact, different style furniture could help to delineate between the informal kitchen and more structured dining areas.

Comfortable chairs are a must if you expect friends and family to sit around a table and take time over a meal. The chairs should be the right height for the table, so that you do not have to lean over or stretch up to a plate, but there is enough room to cross your legs and relax after dining. If the chairs are hard, wood or steel say, you may need to add a pad or cushion. Although they can be less attractive, moulded plastic chairs do tend to have more 'give' and are easy to wipe clean and maintain in what is a sticky and greasy environment.

Opposite **If a seat is to be used for dining, and so will have to support someone for hours at a time, then it should be comfortable. This webbing weave will be more relaxing to sit on than a chair with a hard wooden or solid plastic seat.**
Right **In this minimal monochrome room the colour and style of the chairs is the focal point.**

Above **The contrast between the pale wood and smooth surface of the units and the roughness of the flooring is echoed in the polished surfaces of the chair and the roughness of the table top.**

Right **A high stool is ideal for a breakfast-bar area where snacks rather than main meals are taken.**

Far right **These stools have a steel ring just above the base, providing somewhere to rest your feet. The upholstered seat adds to the comfort factor.**

Opposite **This wall of built-in storage has been divided into deep base drawers with tall shelved cupboards above. The tops of the cupboard doors are infilled with a grid which allows air to circulate and, with the panel detailing, prevent the doors from appearing too solid and bland.**

Right **These high-backed chairs with foot bars provide maximum support and comfort for anyone who is dining at a breakfast bar.**

Far right **This classic country-style kitchen has a traditional plate rack where freshly washed and dried dishes are stored directly above the sink. Not only a practical solution to crockery storage, the rack also enhances the utilitarian appearance of the room. This style of unit, or a wine rack, can be custom-made to fit into an awkward gap between two standard-size, factory-made units.**

Below **Rattan or Lloyd Loom chairs have a certain amount of 'give', making them comfortable to sit on for long periods. They are also lightweight and easy to move around.**

When choosing high stools for a breakfast bar think of comfort. For example, if the stool does not have a rung or foot rest on the base of the legs, your legs may get tired dangling around in the air, so it may be wise to add a rail on the side of the bar, or to find a suitable stool that has a rail incorporated in its design. In general, stools can also be taxing on the back. It is more relaxing to have some form of lower lumbar support, although this comfort may have to be sacrificed if the stool is to be stored under a worktop.

Tables come in all sorts of shapes and sizes and they should be chosen to suit the rest of the furnishings in the room, as well as in a size and dimension that is appropriate. All tables in kitchen areas should be easy to wipe clean and if the area is dual purpose or small, a table with folding ends may be useful, so that the table size can be reduced when not in use, but elongated for dining or food preparation for a large gathering. When choosing a table, beware of buying one with too many or badly positioned legs. The legs may look like an attractive feature in the shop but think of the practicalities of seating six or eight people around it, and consider that someone may have to sit astride the legs during such a gathering. For small kitchens, look at the possibilities of foldaway furniture. Some small tables can be attached to the wall and let down flush with the wall when not in use. Chairs that fold flat can be stored in a cupboard or in another room, to be brought out when needed.

Whatever you choose, make sure that it is suitable for a kitchen, in particular that it can be easily cleaned. Grand padded chairs with fabric upholstery will soon be stained or splashed in this bustling, busy environment.

Above, above right and right **It can be easier to buy the stool and then adjust the height of the worktop, rather than trying to find stools to accommodate the worktop height.**
Top right **Classic fine beech wood chairs like these are flexible enough to offer comfort.**
Far right and opposite below **A table with adjustable extra leaves is a bonus when entertaining.**
Opposite above **A large upholstered sofa defines where the kitche area ends and the lounging area begins.**

display

Decoration can be applied to a kitchen in many ways: there does not need to be a great riot of frills, patterns and artefacts for there to be embellishment – in fact unnecessary clutter will only attract grease and grime and add to the task of cleaning. Utilitarian and simple objects can be attractive if they are well ordered. In Simple Modern and New Professional kitchens gilt-framed pictures, fancy curtains and ornate china will look out of place, yet decoration can be included so long as the items are in keeping with their surroundings.

For example, in a minimalist kitchen a glass shelf of strictly regimented glasses can be interesting, and immaculate chrome canisters will also be eye catching. Glass shelves give a feeling of lightness, as though the objects on them were floating rather than set solidly on a wooden shelf. But when there are only a few items on show they have to be perfect, clean and polished. If there is little to attract the eye elsewhere they become the focus of attention. A directional spotlamp can be used to highlight simple displays, such as a row of glasses, when the rest of the room is illuminated by candles or low-level light. Or, if it is placed near a window, the display will be illuminated by daylight, which will accentuate the sparkle and reflections on the glass.

Opposite **Simple everyday items can look attractive if well displayed.**
Top left **Shiny items such as chrome canisters should be sparkling, not smudged with greasy finger marks.**
Above **Polished glassware always looks appealing.**
Left **Choose items to put on show that are appropriate to the overall theme or scheme of the kitchen.**

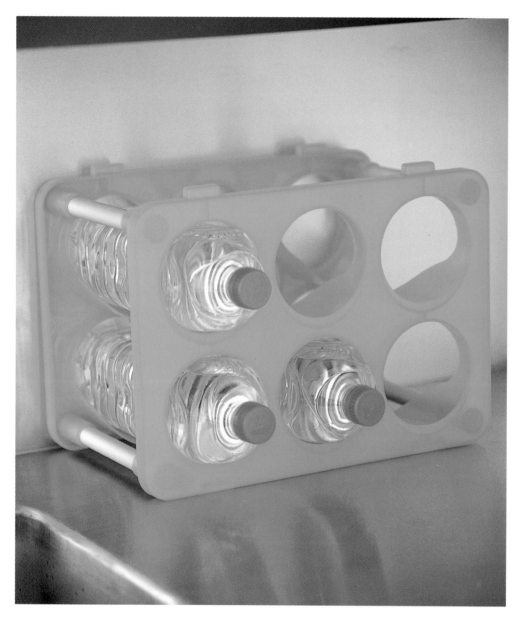

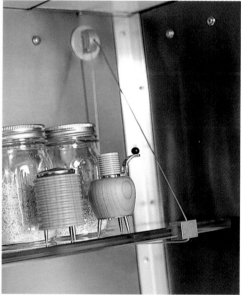

Above **In a plain or monotone scheme a single bright object like this vivid plastic bottle rack will become a focal point.**

Top right **A single unexpected item or objects can attract the eye.**

Above right **A glass shelf makes the objects on it appear to be suspended in the air.**

Opposite **Soften a clinical steel façade with a single bloom.**

When placing objects in groups on a shelf it can be interesting to split them into clusters of three or five – somehow odd numbers look more interesting than groups made up from even numbers of objects. White plates on a plate rack can be grouped so that the different sizes of plates create a pattern, for example a group of dinner plates followed by a similar number of side plates, a few more dinner plates and then some bowls.

A single unexpected item amongst a line of compatible objects can also be appealing. For example, a coloured glass among a row of plain glasses, a wicker whisk in a line of metal fish slices. The juxtaposition of a simple curved vase

against a background of angular knives or unit doors will also be of interest in a room where there is little other decoration.

Fresh fruit and vegetables, the very ingredients of meals to be cooked, can in themselves be decorative objects. A dark wood bowl filled with polished red apples, a wicker basket laden with speckled brown eggs, bottles of oil with chillies or herbs suspended in the rich yellow green liquid are all appealing and appropriate to the location.

Storage containers can also be attractive – a brightly coloured plastic wine rack will bring order to a jumble of wine bottles and its colour and shape may be pleasing. Wire or wicker baskets

filled with comestibles can also be left on display. Cutlery, shiny and silvery, can be made to appear inviting and interesting if stored in an old wooden tray or in bundles in pots or jars. Old knives and forks with ornate handles or polished yellowy bone handles can be stored blade down so that the handles splay out like the bones of a fan.

In Traditional and Simple Country kitchens the style is more appropriate to arrangements of plates and china, especially on dressers or open shelves. In fifties-style kitchens old enamelware and early Denby china is appropriate – the simple classic lines of enamelled plates, bowls and jugs are pleasing to the eye and the decorative china will help emphasize the theme and period of the decor.

Country style need not be cluttered but it does encourage the spirit of industry and collecting – jars of homemade jams and pickles, bunches of dried herbs over the hearth or fireplace. Cushions on old wooden chairs, gingham tablecloths and napkins add softness and comfort. But a little can go a long way – too many baskets and bunches of flowers, rows of china bowls and heaps of baking trays may make it look as though you are running a shop rather than an efficient and hygienic kitchen.

Where the displays are arranged is important. If the items are frequently used, like glasses and tableware, then they can be left on open shelves because they will be in and out of the dishwasher or washing-up bowl regularly. Glass shelves are handsome, but must be kept dust free so a couple of them may be enough; a special feature rather than the norm. Cabinets with glass panels in the doors will allow items to be seen but provide a barrier between them and the steam and smoke of the kitchen. Worktop areas are really the hub of kitchen activity and should be kept as uncluttered and clean as possible, but a few good-looking items can be positioned to the back of the worktop or in areas that are less frequently used.

There is an oriental custom that in the wall of the main living room there is a small niche, and under the niche is a chest. The chest contains the family's treasures and each day a single treasure is taken out and displayed in the niche. The single item, a vase or bowl maybe, can then be appreciated without the distraction of other ornaments. This 'less is more' philosophy can be applied to any plainly decorated room – even the kitchen.

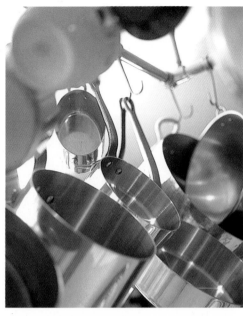

Opposite, clockwise from top left **Arrangements of goods in neat wire baskets create an appealing symmetry. Cutlery old or new can be displayed.** This page, clockwise from top left **Different shapes and sizes of the same item, such as gleaming copper pans sending out endless reflections of themselves, add architectural interest in an otherwise well-ordered room. A modern knife block with a graceful metal stand is an attractive and safe way of storing knives. Instead of having a motley collection of bags of flour and sugar, decant the contents into matching tins or jars. Open-shelf display is good for items that are used regularly. Even plates on a drying rack can be pleasingly arranged. China shapes do not have to be identical – as long as they are of the same colour they will sit happily together on a shelf. Uneven numbers of objects make interesting groups. Variety can bring interest: display utensils together in tall pots.**

dec

oration
colour flooring

introduction

Decoration can be a way of reviving and revitalizing an existing kitchen and an opportunity of bringing a more fashionable note to a classic or traditional setting. If you are starting from scratch, certain schemes and colourways may already have been suggested by the type and style of units you have chosen to install. The size and shape of the room and the amount of natural light available may also influence your choice.

Decoration involves a number of different finishes and materials, from paints and ceramic tiles to soft furnishings such as curtains, blinds, seat cushions and table cloths. To give the whole room a cohesive look it is wise to plan your decorative scheme throughout before putting paint on the wall or buying metres of fabric. As with the general planning of the layout of the kitchen it is a good idea to keep a notebook of decorating ideas. A simple paper back schoolbook or similar can be used to staple samples of material in, and to keep colour cards from paint manufacturers and photographs and clippings from magazines. If you are good at drawing you may also want to sketch in ideas that you see or feel you could adapt to suit your setting. The book can also be used to keep a list of measurements handy, for example, for windows and floor areas, so that you can gauge the costs of materials when you chance upon something you like – this sort of comparison will help you keep an eye on your budget. This reference book will prove invaluable when you start to work out your scheme, whether you do it yourself or with the help of a professional decorator, as it is easier to show examples of a colour or a curtain finish than it is to try to describe it in words.

The actual materials used for decorating will vary in type and availability of colour. For example, the tough and efficient surfaces – the worktops, splashbacks and floors – come in a more limited range of colour than the paint for the wall. Therefore, when choosing the 'colourful' parts of the scheme make sure that they blend and sit comfortably with the less colourful but 'useful' elements. Do not be too dogmatic or rigid about your selection as you may be disappointed if you cannot track down just the right shade of bright green work surface. Remember too much of one colour can be overpowering; try different shades of a colour or contrast it with a brighter or darker colour for variety. Look at texture as well. The type of materials that you might use – smooth ceramic tiles or opaque glass bricks – can be contrasted with roughly woven linen, brick or grained wood. Various textures have different effects and the combination of smooth and rough can create visual interest in a plainly coloured scheme.

Opposite **Choosing the decoration for your kitchen gives you the opportunity to explore an abundance of colours, textures and materials.**

colour

Colours for kitchens can be divided into four main groups. The first category is the cool spectrum of blue, green, grey; secondly there are the hot shades – red, orange, sunshine yellow; then the dramatic colours are the rich reds, deep purples and black; and finally there are the pastels, a title that covers beige, soft pink, baby blue and pale primrose yellow.

When mixing colours it is often useful to refer to the three primary colours: red, blue, and yellow. Using these colours as a base you can work out a safe combination for a scheme. For example, if you mix blue and yellow you get green, and as a basic rule of thumb blue, yellow and green are compatible in something like a fabric print or a ceramic tile pattern. Red and yellow make orange, so again those three colours are likely to be harmonious, as are red, blue and their offspring purple.

Using darker and lighter shades of a colour can also be used to interesting effect and is often referred to by professional decorators as 'tone on tone'. For example, plain units may be painted in a mid grey, the skirting board, door frames and kickboard panel under the units could be in mid-charcoal tone, with a similar shade of granite for the worktop, and the walls painted in the faintest hint of pearl grey. A steel sink and drainer, silvery taps and chrome accessories would all work well against this setting, but add unexpected splashes of colour – such as a fuchsia-pink table cloth, a row of bold terracotta

Opposite **Details are an important ingredient in the overall decoration; shining handles on a plain painted cabinet give a lift to its appearance.**
Above **Choose colours that are appropriate to the style or period of decoration you are following.**
Right **The colour of a shelf or cabinet can act as a contrasting background and can highlight the objects displayed on or in it.**
Far right **By painting a single piece of furniture in a different colour from the walls you will make it stand out and give it more impact.**

and black ethnic plates and jars or a couple of bright red enamel casseroles – to prevent the whole thing from becoming bland or dull.

Lighting and colour

The type of light used in a room can also change the appearance of a colour. The intensity of the colour often changes depending on whether it is viewed in natural or artificial light, so, if possible, paint an area of wall with the colour you have in mind, or pin up a swatch of the fabric you propose to use for the curtains or soft furnishings, and live with it for a few days. Look at the colours in daylight, again at dusk and then under artificial light. Dark colours become denser as the day progresses and what might seem like a strong but interesting colour on a bright summer's morning may become gloomy and oppressive on a dark winter's day. A sunny yellow paint may be great in daylight but become acidic or 'dirty' in electric light. Also, check fabrics and paints together, since items that appear to be a good match under the fluorescent rays of a shop light fitting can look quite different when you get them home, or in daylight. Blue lights, such as fluorescents, can have a dramatic effect on some of the more modern acid colours, so these shades should always be checked against other colours in the room and in the full range of light sources to be used in the room.

The way in which colour is distributed is also important. A dark ceiling and pale walls will make the ceiling appear lower. Dark skirting boards and

Left **This kitchen is painted in a hot vivid orange that makes the flag-floored room seem warm even in the depth of winter. The original stone surround to the fireplace has been lined with stainless steel and is used to house a modern professional-style cooker and grill.**

Top left **Although the colour is contemporary many of the objects displayed against it are traditional; the choice and arrangement of the items make old and new compatible.**

Top right and above **A rail of gleaming utensils and the chrome and glass storage is highlighted by the strong wall colour.**

Opposite **The dark muted blue of the back wall accentuates the chrome extractor pipe, clock and pale panelled plank door.**
Below **The blue wall butts up to the white side walls and ceiling, chrome worktops and pale sanded wood flooring, making a feature out of the darker expanse of wall.**
Right **A rich warm colour like this yellow can brighten a dark or basement kitchen. It also suits darker shades of wood.**
Below right **White accessories look clean and fresh against the strongly coloured walls.**

a richly coloured floor will make the floor appear closer. Darker painted details such as door and window frames, against a pale wall or pale units will make the details stand out, so if you are high-lighting these features make sure that they are of a quality and finish that will withstand scrutiny and are worthy of the accolade.

Structural emphasis

High ceilings and tall walls can be reduced by divid-ing the wall into different areas and painting them different colours. This technique works particularly well in period rooms. The ceiling can be painted in a mid tone, beneath that a picture rail can be added at about 30 cm (1 ft) from the top of the wall, and the area between the ceiling and the rail painted in white. The wall beneath the rail to the dado rail, which is approximately 90 cm (3 ft) from the floor, can be painted in the same colour as the

ceiling. The dado rail itself can be picked out with white paint and beneath that a much deeper shade. This division will help reduce the size of the room and also has the practical effect of making the room bright (with the white and pale colours) but the area where chairs, boots and bags may scuff is dark and so less likely to show up marks.

If the room is an uneven shape – perhaps due to an extension added to an existing house or an apartment that has been created by subdividing rooms – then using a variety of shades and colours on the different sections of the wall will not only add interest but may also help to even out the over-all appearance. For example, if a wall has a recess you could choose to ignore it and paint it the same colour as the rest of the walls or you could paint it it a richer or brighter colour and make it a point of interest. If the main walls are a rich raspberry red, the recess could be painted in a harmonious shade

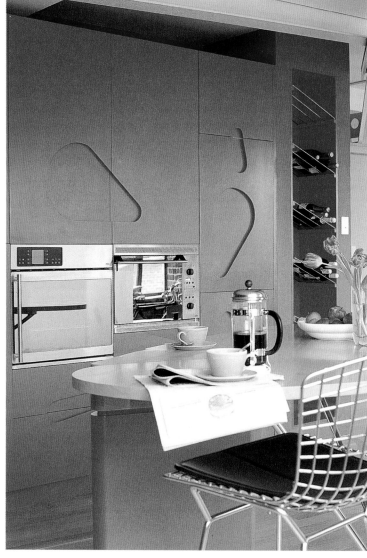

This page **The flame-red façades of these units are cooled by the areas of icy-looking opaque glass, silvery steel furniture and watery-blue china and glassware. The fronts of the doors have also been sculpted so that there are areas of pattern and light and shade, which also reduces the overall impact of the colour.**
Opposite **Different colours can be used to identify the contents of various storage areas: red for frying pans, green for vegetable steamers, for example. As this vibrant mix shows, colours that are different but of similar tones or strengths can sit comfortably side by side.**

of reddish brown, giving a luxurious feel and creating a change of emphasis. Using a deeper shade than the main wall will also create the optical illusion that the recess is deeper, whereas painting it a lighter and brighter shade will make it appear more shallow.

Creating a style

The combination of colour and style is very important, especially if you are following a particular look. For example, vivid orange and acid green are associated with a more contemporary range of colours and would

look out of place in a period kitchen, whereas New Professional or Simply Modern kitchens with clean stainless steel units and simple tiling can act as a foil to almost any colour.

Another deciding factor may be that you have chosen a particular fabric for curtains, cushions or cloths. The colours within the pattern of the textile may give you a starting point for your decorative scheme. But do remember if the room is small and dark paler shades will make it look more spacious, so if the curtain fabric is dark choose a lighter tone of one of the darker colours.

Above **Manmade materials such as Melamine and Formica come in a wide choice of plain colors and designs; they may mimic nature with wood and marble effects or feature complex patterns such as this.** Above right, clockwise from top left **Pop-style glasses pick up the Op Art surface design. Sculptural chairs follow the theme. Plain stainless-steel backsplashes and cabinets balance the areas of pattern.** Opposite **This complex pattern of black line drawings appears gray from a distance; since the unit surfaces and table are so densely decorated, the rest of the scheme is plain to provide a balance.**

If the kitchen units are in natural wood most colours will be suitable, either in a similar tone or in direct contrast. If the units are already painted, lacquered or stained, then the colour chosen for the rest of the room should be selected with the unit colour in mind, as they tend to be a dominant feature in a kitchen.

For example, if you opt for a bright blue finish to the units a subtle burnt orange wash on the walls or a paler turquoise blue matt finish paint can make the scheme modern and vibrant. The same units set against plain white walls may give it a more Mediterranean feel, which could be accentuated with accessories such as simple hand-painted ceramics and plain terracotta plates and bowls. The same units again, but this time with

yellow walls and simple blue, white and yellow striped soft furnishing could hint of the scheme found at the Impressionist artist Claude Monet's house in France.

Lack of colour can also be an interesting feature. If you have a plain white kitchen with pale wood or steel fittings the accessories you add will be features. The lack of colour in the scheme will also make it timeless and if the walls are simply white they will be easily touched up or re-painted when the surfaces begin to look a little worn or damaged.

Black is an interesting colour, but one that many people avoid in kitchens. Black can make a room seem small and stuffy, but used in carefully controlled amounts, it can be very dramatic. For example, an

item in the kitchen that is a necessity but not necessarily an asset to the room, like a radiator, could be cased in and painted black, so that it becomes featureless. Kickboards under units will seem to disappear if painted black and matt black walls can double as giant blackboards on which shopping lists, poems and phone numbers can be scribbled.

Black detailing can be used to accentuate the shape and design of a piece of furniture or an architectural feature in the room. This emphasis can be done within the edge of a door panel or at the edge of a drawer or cupboard to create the impression of a frame. Black on natural wood is very effective, but the same result can be achieved with other dark contrasting colours, such as navy or grey.

flooring

Opposite **A simple chequerboard pattern is traditional in black and white, but it can be brought up to date by using different colours.**
Left **On either side of this work unit and sink are insets of red brick paviours in a blocked pattern, which contrasts with the borders, façades, surfaces and steps, which are in white marble.**
Below **This striped effect is achieved with three tones of laminate floor covering which contrast with the solid colour of the units.**

The priority for a kitchen floor covering is that it should be a safe, non-slip surface and easy to clean. There are many types of flooring to choose from, but remember that the finished floor will only be as good as the surface beneath it. Make sure that the base onto which the floor will be laid is clean, even and well prepared, otherwise the faults will be magnified when the flooring is laid.

Tile and stone

Floor tiles must not to be confused with those intended for work surface use. They are thicker and larger, and are made to withstand the wear and tear of being underfoot. There are two categories: natural and decorative. Natural tiles are made with different types of baked clay – terracotta tiles are

the most common. Their colour depends on the clay used: it can vary from rich red to creamier tones. Quarry tiles, made from durable unrefined aluminium clay, are high fired and less porous than many other types of clay tile. Prices for these tiles vary. Hand-made tiles are the most expensive, but some manufacturers mechanically produce tiles with a slightly irregular look which will create the same overall effect less expensively.

Although not technically a tile, bricks are made of clay and fired, so may be included in this section. Bricks come in a range of colours, from creamy-brown to traditional red and those with blue and purple hues. This comparatively cheap and hardwearing material can be laid in herringbone and other patterns or in simple rows.

Decorative tiles are generally glazed ceramic shapes, usually square, but sometimes oblong or hexagonal. These tiles can have a high sheen or a matt finish, and come in a rainbow assortment of colours and patterns. They are easy to clean but may be slippery underfoot if a spillage occurs. Ceramic tiles may also break if a heavy object is dropped on them; the broken or cracked tile can be replaced but it is a difficult job to remove a single tile when it is grouted. Ceramic tiles offer infinite opportunities to create patterns and mix colours, from simple chequerboards to complex designs.

Marble, granite, slate, limestone, Yorkstone and sandstone all come in the category of stone. The slabs or tiles are larger than the average ceramic tile and because they are heavy they are

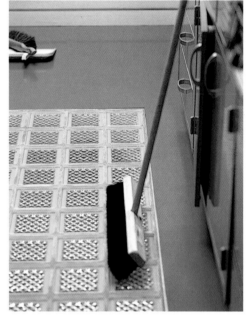

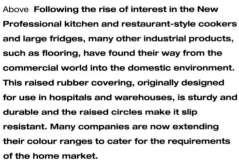

Above **Following the rise of interest in the New Professional kitchen and restaurant-style cookers and large fridges, many other industrial products, such as flooring, have found their way from the commercial world into the domestic environment. This raised rubber covering, originally designed for use in hospitals and warehouses, is sturdy and durable and the raised circles make it slip resistant. Many companies are now extending their colour ranges to cater for the requirements of the home market.**

Above right **Heavy-duty textured glass bricks, which are often used in pavements or outside walls to bring light into basements, have been used here to create a small mat-like inset into the tiled floor. They make an unusual but practical floor covering.**

Right **Textured linoleum is practical and easy to clean and is warm underfoot.**

Opposite **This floor is covered in a staggered pattern of Italian tiles which are cool and hard, but waterproof and simple to mop clean.**

best used on ground-level floors. These rigid and often uneven stones can be difficult to lay, and this may be best done by a professional. A stone floor is hard wearing and will withstand any amount of wear, tear and water. The disadvantages are that it is cold under foot (though this can be counteracted by underfloor heating) and very hard. China and glass dropped on a stone floor will invariably break, whereas on softer surfaces there is a chance it would survive intact.

Marble comes in a wide range of colours and types, from the classic white Italian with grey veins to rich reds and greens such as Irish Connemara varieties. Marble can be expensive if you buy solid tiles, but if you opt for a thin veneer of marble laid on a cement or concrete base you can keep the cost down. It is solid and easy to maintain, but a marble floor may become slippery when wet.

Sheet and soft flooring

Linoleum is made from linseed oil, finely ground wood flour and pine resin, with a jute backing. Fashionable in the 1940s and '50s, it has in recent years seen a steady revival. Often referred to as 'lino', it comes in rolls and easier-to-manage tiles. It is easy to brush and mop clean, and if required a polish or finish can be applied.

Vinyl is lino's brighter and more versatile younger sister. It is a chemically based product, with an infinite range of colours and patterns. It is

Above and right **Two different types of flooring have been used here – wood and slate – and the zig zag edge where the two floors meet echos the irregular join of the plaster ceiling and glass extension. By using two different types of flooring definition can be given to different areas in the same room, wood in the kitchen and slate in the dining/seating area.**
Opposite **Wood is an attractive and warm floor covering but it should be well sealed and finished to prevent water and wear damage. Wooden planks and parquet can be laid in many ways to form patterns and optical effects that can make a room appear longer or wider.**

hardwearing and long lasting, but for all its good qualities it is worth noting that the surface will be effected by burns and grit which will mark the top layer. Some types of vinyl flooring have to be sealed with a recommended finish, but this need only be applied two or three times a year, even in a busy traffic area. Cushioned vinyl has a soft, slightly spongy backing. Sometimes patterns are stamped into the two layers, giving the motif a three-dimensional appearance. If heavy furniture rests on this type of floor it will dent the surface, so to avoid permanent damage put protective cups or shields over the leg ends.

Rubber usually comes from industrial sources and should be laid on a concrete or similarly smooth, solid base. Available in a range of colours and raised relief patterns, rubber floors are very good in a contemporary setting.

Cork's warm, soft surface has made it a popular floor covering for many years, and as there are floor and wall quality tiles it is best to check that you are getting the right type. Tiles are usually impregnated with a polyurethane seal to make them more resistant to water; check they are sealed before you lay them. Although the natural golden honey colour of plain cork tiles has been perennially popular, manufacturers now supply cork in a range of colours which can be used to create different patterns and effects.

Coir or sisal matting, made from natural fibres such as coconut husk and the agave leaves, is hardwearing and, if pre-treated, can be stain resistant, but it should not be used near a sink or cooker where it may come into contact with excess water, a spark or fat. Make sure you have an effective vacuum cleaner as food trapped in this type of matting can be difficult to remove ,and may in extreme cases decay and lead to ant infestation.

Wood

Wood makes an attractive and timeless flooring. There are so many different varieties and colours of wood, as well as ways of laying it, that there is a type of wooden floor to suit every style of kitchen design. Whether you opt for plain boards laid in parallel lines, parquet with its tighter geometric design or patterns, such as herringbone laid in an interconnecting 'V' construction, there is a way of laying a wooden floor to suit most tastes. The versatility of wood goes beyond the designs that can be achieved in its laying; it also has wide colour prospects too. It can be left natural, enhanced with a little wax or varnish, or stained to a richer darker hue, or painted in primary colours with decorative borders or given a pale, subtle colourwash.

There are two main families of wood – hard and soft. Hard woods such as elm, walnut, ash, oak and maple tend to be in the upper price bracket and in some cases are rare or difficult to procure because they are environmentally protected species, and they should only be bought if they can be accredited as coming from managed forests. Soft woods, such as pine, are invariably from managed woods. These trees take less time to grow and are a more easily renewable source. Pine is cheaper than hard woods and is more economical to use if you are going to paint or stain the floor. You can use basic emulsion or marine paint, which is very durable, but it takes a long time to dry and comes in a limited range of colours. All wood floors, whether natural, stained or painted, need to be sealed in a kitchen environment. There are various types, from wax polish, matt and polyurethane varnish to high-gloss deck varnish, but it is important to choose the right type of finish to suit the rest of your scheme.